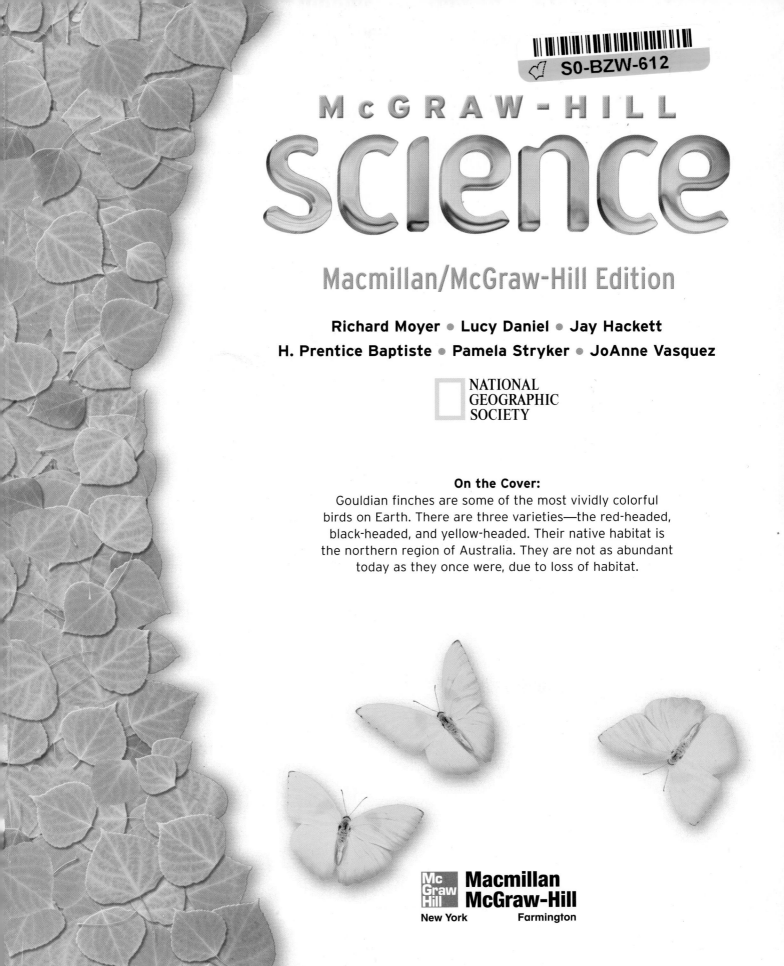

S0-BZW-612

McGRAW-HILL
SCIENCE

Macmillan/McGraw-Hill Edition

Richard Moyer • Lucy Daniel • Jay Hackett
H. Prentice Baptiste • Pamela Stryker • JoAnne Vasquez

NATIONAL
GEOGRAPHIC
SOCIETY

On the Cover:
Gouldian finches are some of the most vividly colorful
birds on Earth. There are three varieties—the red-headed,
black-headed, and yellow-headed. Their native habitat is
the northern region of Australia. They are not as abundant
today as they once were, due to loss of habitat.

Mc Graw Hill **Macmillan**
McGraw-Hill

New York   Farmington

Program Authors

Dr. Lucy H. Daniel
Teacher, Consultant
Rutherford County Schools, North Carolina

Dr. Jay Hackett
Professor Emeritus of Earth Sciences
University of Northern Colorado

Dr. Richard H. Moyer
Professor of Science Education
University of Michigan-Dearborn

Dr. H. Prentice Baptiste
Professor of Science and Multicultural Education
New Mexico State University
Las Cruces, New Mexico

Pamela Stryker, M.Ed.
Elementary Educator and Science Consultant
Eanes Independent School District
Austin, Texas

Dr. JoAnne Vasquez
Elementary Science Education Consultant
Mesa Public Schools, Arizona
NSTA Past President

learning through listening

Students with print disabilities may be eligible to obtain an accessible, audio version of the pupil edition of this textbook. Please call Recording for the Blind & Dyslexic at 1-800-221-4792 for complete information.

NATIONAL GEOGRAPHIC SOCIETY

Washington, D.C.

The features in this textbook entitled "Invitation to Science," "Amazing Stories," and "People in Science," as well as the unit openers, were developed in collaboration with the National Geographic Society's School Publishing Division.

Macmillan/McGraw-Hill

A Division of The **McGraw·Hill** Companies

Published by Macmillan/McGraw-Hill, of McGraw-Hill Education, a division of The McGraw-Hill Companies, Inc., Two Penn Plaza, New York, New York 10121.

Printed in the United States of America

ISBN 0-02-280057-3 / 3

1 2 3 4 5 6 7 8 9 058 07 06 05 04 03 02

Life Science

Consultants

Dr. Carol Baskin
University of Kentucky
Lexington, KY

Dr. Joe W. Crim
University of Georgia
Athens, GA

Dr. Marie DiBerardino
Allegheny University of
Health Sciences
Philadelphia, PA

Dr. R. E. Duhrkopf
Baylor University
Waco, TX

Dr. Dennis L. Nelson
Montana State University
Bozeman, MT

Dr. Fred Sack
Ohio State University
Columbus, OH

Dr. Martin VanDyke
Denver, CO

Dr. E. Peter Volpe
Mercer University
Macon, GA

Earth Science

Consultants

Dr. Clarke Alexander
Skidaway Institute of
Oceanography
Savannah, GA

Dr. Suellen Cabe
Pembroke State University
Pembroke, NC

Dr. Thomas A. Davies
Texas A & M University
College Station, TX

Dr. Ed Geary
Geological Society of America
Boulder, CO

Dr. David C. Kopaska-Merkel
Geological Survey of Alabama
Tuscaloosa, AL

Physical Science

Consultants

Dr. Bonnie Buratti
Jet Propulsion Lab
Pasadena, CA

Dr. Shawn Carlson
Society of Amateur Scientists
San Diego, CA

Dr. Karen Kwitter
Williams College
Williamstown, MA

Dr. Steven Souza
Williamstown, MA

Dr. Joseph P. Straley
University of Kentucky
Lexington, KY

Dr. Thomas Troland
University of Kentucky
Lexington, KY

Dr. Josephine Davis Wallace
University of North Carolina
Charlotte, NC

Consultant for Primary Grades

Donna Harrell Lubcker
East Texas Baptist University
Marshall, TX

Teacher Panelists

Newark, NJ
First Avenue School
Jorge Alameda
Concetta Cioci
Neva Galasso
Bernadette Kazanjian-reviewer
Toby Marks
Janet Mayer-reviewer
Maria Tutela

Brooklyn, NY
P.S. 31
Janet Mantel
Paige McGlone
Madeline Pappas
Maria Puma-reviewer
P.S. 217
Rosemary Ahern
Charles Brown
Claudia Deeb-reviewer
Wendy Lerner
P.S. 225
Christine Calafiore
Annette Fisher-reviewer

P.S. 250
Melissa Kane
P.S. 277
Erica Cohen
Helena Conti
Anne Marie Corrado
Deborah Scott-DiClemente
Jeanne Fish
Diane Fromhartz
Tricia Hinz
Lisa Iside
Susan Malament
Joyce Menkes-reviewer
Elaine Noto
Jean Pennacchio
Jeffrey Hampton
Mwaka Yavana

Elmont, NY
Covert Avenue School
Arlene Connelly

Mt. Vernon, NY
Holmes School
Jennifer Cavallaro
Lou Ciofi
George DiFiore
Brenda Durante
Jennifer Hawkins-reviewer
Michelle Mazzotta
Catherine Moringiello
Mary Jane Oria-reviewer
Lucille Pierotti
Pia Vicario-reviewer

Ozone Park, NY
St. Elizabeth School
Joanne Cocchiola-reviewer
Helen DiPietra-reviewer
Barbara Kingston
Madeline Visco

St. Albans, NY
Orvia Williams

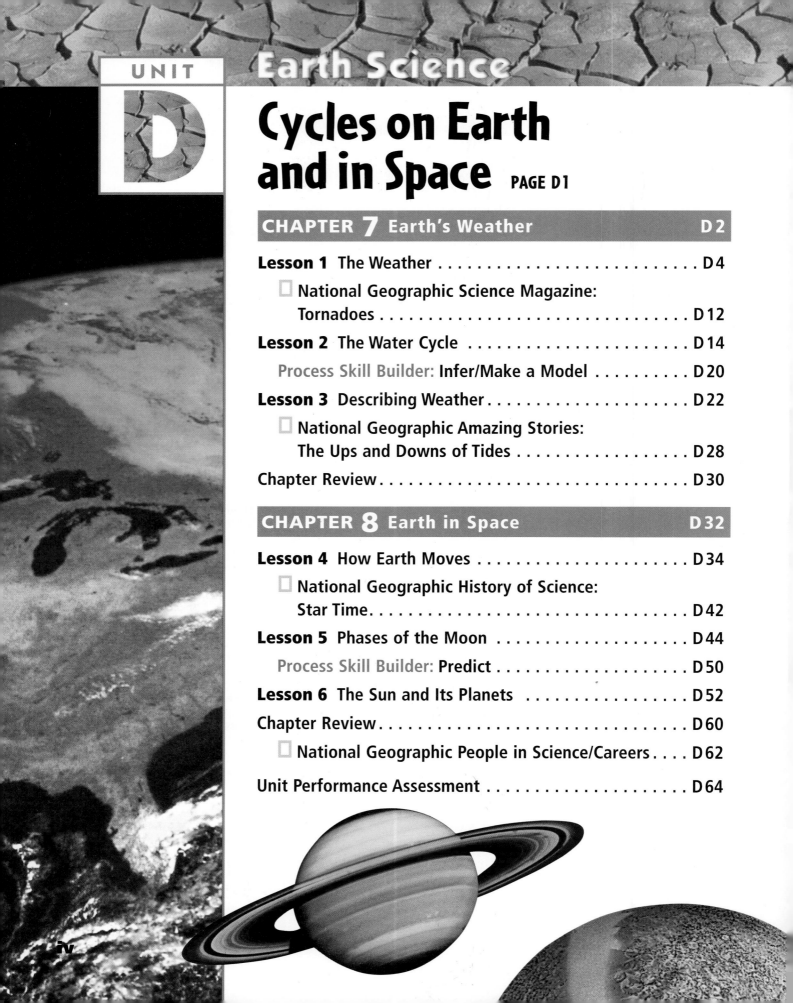

Cycles on Earth and in Space PAGE D1

As you study science, you will learn many new words. You will read about many new ideas. Read these pages. They will help you understand this book.

1. The **Vocabulary** list has all the new words you will learn in the lesson. The page numbers tell you where the words are taught.

2. The name tells you what the lesson is about.

3. **Get Ready** uses the picture on the page to help you start thinking about the lesson.

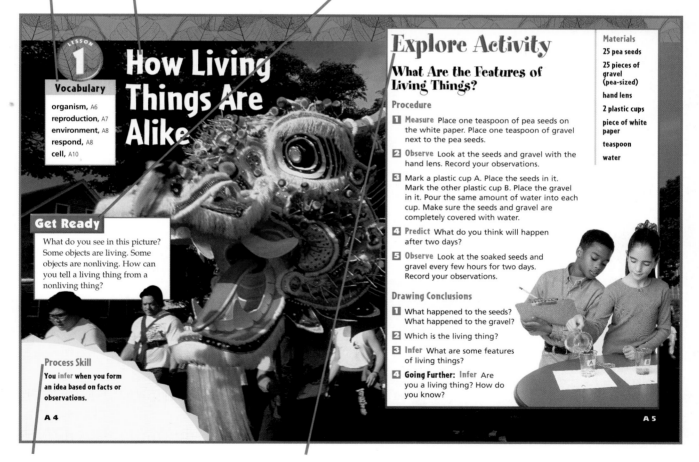

LESSON
1

How Living Things Are Alike

Vocabulary

organism, A6
reproduction, A7
environment, A8
respond, A8
cell, A10

Get Ready

What do you see in this picture? Some objects are living. Some objects are nonliving. How can you tell a living thing from a nonliving thing?

Process Skill

You infer when you form an idea based on facts or observations.

A 4

Explore Activity

What Are the Features of Living Things?

Procedure

1 **Measure** Place one teaspoon of pea seeds on the white paper. Place one teaspoon of gravel next to the pea seeds.

2 **Observe** Look at the seeds and gravel with the hand lens. Record your observations.

3 Mark a plastic cup A. Place the seeds in it. Mark the other plastic cup B. Place the gravel in it. Pour the same amount of water into each cup. Make sure the seeds and gravel are completely covered with water.

4 **Predict** What do you think will happen after two days?

5 **Observe** Look at the soaked seeds and gravel every few hours for two days. Record your observations.

Drawing Conclusions

1 What happened to the seeds? What happened to the gravel?

2 Which is the living thing?

3 **Infer** What are some features of living things?

4 **Going Further: Infer** Are you a living thing? How do you know?

Materials

25 pea seeds
25 pieces of gravel (pea-sized)
hand lens
2 plastic cups
piece of white paper
teaspoon
water

A 5

4. This **Process Skill** is used in the Explore Activity.

5. The **Explore Activity** is a hands-on way to learn about the lesson.

As you read a lesson, follow these three steps. They will help you to understand what you are reading.

1. This box contains the **Main Idea** of the lesson. Keep the main idea of the lesson in mind as you read.

2. Before Reading Read the large red question before you read the page. Try to answer this question from what you already know.

3. During Reading Look for new **Vocabulary** words in yellow. Look at the pictures. They will help you understand what you are reading.

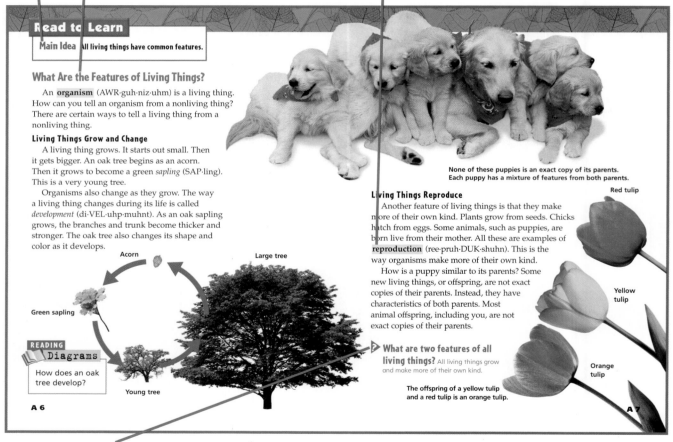

Read to Learn

Main Idea All living things have common features.

What Are the Features of Living Things?

An **organism** (AWR·guh·niz·uhm) is a living thing. How can you tell an organism from a nonliving thing? There are certain ways to tell a living thing from a nonliving thing.

Living Things Grow and Change

A living thing grows. It starts out small. Then it gets bigger. An oak tree begins as an acorn. Then it grows to become a green *sapling* (SAP·ling). This is a very young tree.

Organisms also change as they grow. The way a living thing changes during its life is called *development* (di·VEL·uhp·muhnt). As an oak sapling grows, the branches and trunk become thicker and stronger. The oak tree also changes its shape and color as it develops.

Acorn

Green sapling

Large tree

READING
Diagrams
How does an oak tree develop?

Young tree

A 6

None of these puppies is an exact copy of its parents. Each puppy has a mixture of features from both parents.

Living Things Reproduce

Another feature of living things is that they make more of their own kind. Plants grow from seeds. Chicks hatch from eggs. Some animals, such as puppies, are born live from their mother. All these are examples of **reproduction** (ree·pruh·DUK·shuhn). This is the way organisms make more of their own kind.

How is a puppy similar to its parents? Some new living things, or offspring, are not exact copies of their parents. Instead, they have characteristics of both parents. Most animal offspring, including you, are not exact copies of their parents.

▷ **What are two features of all living things?** All living things grow and make more of their own kind.

The offspring of a yellow tulip and a red tulip is an orange tulip.

Red tulip

Yellow tulip

Orange tulip

A 7

4. After Reading ▷ This arrow points to a question. It will help you check that you understand what you have read. Try to answer the question before you go to the next large red question.

UNIT D

Cycles on Earth and in Space

NATIONAL GEOGRAPHIC

Cycles on Earth and in Space

LOOK!

The Moon moves around Earth. How do you think Earth moves through space

CHAPTER

7

Earth's Weather

Did You Ever Wonder?

How does snow form? Snow is not frozen rain.
Snow forms when water in the gas state, called
water vapor, changes directly into ice crystals. As
the crystals fall to Earth, they combine to form
snowflakes. No two snowflakes are alike. How
does water get into the air?

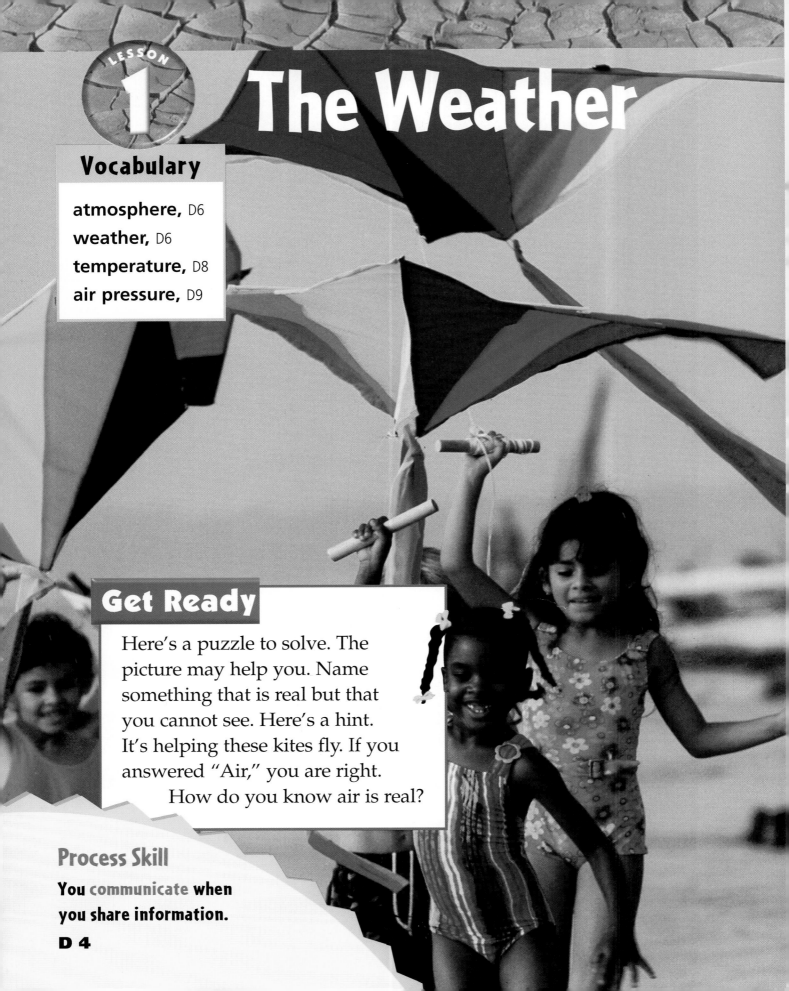

The Weather

Vocabulary

atmosphere, D6
weather, D6
temperature, D8
air pressure, D9

Get Ready

Here's a puzzle to solve. The picture may help you. Name something that is real but that you cannot see. Here's a hint. It's helping these kites fly. If you answered "Air," you are right.

How do you know air is real?

Process Skill

You communicate when you share information.

Explore Activity

How Can You Show That Air Is Real?

Materials

plastic container

plastic cup

water

paper towels

Procedure

1 Fill the container about half full with water.

2 Put a dry paper towel completely inside the cup.

3 Hold the cup upside down. Push the cup to the bottom of the container. Be careful not to tilt the cup.

4 **Observe** Remove the cup from the water. Remember to be careful not to tilt the cup. Look at the towel. Record your findings.

5 **Observe** Again, hold the cup upside down, and push it to the bottom of the container. This time slowly tilt the cup. Record your findings.

Drawing Conclusions

1 What happened to the towel in step 3? In step 5?

2 What was inside the cup?

3 Is air real? How can you tell?

4 **Going Further: Communicate** What other senses did you use as you tilted the cup and air bubbles escaped?

Main Idea Three characteristics of the weather are air temperature, air pressure, and wind.

Where Is Air?

How can you tell if air is real? Wave a plastic sandwich bag around, and close it. There is something in the bag. That something is air. Now open the bag, and flatten it out. Close the bag. Where did the air go?

Air is all around you. Air surrounds the entire Earth. The air that surrounds Earth is called the **atmosphere** (AT·muhs·feer). The atmosphere is made up of different gases and dust. Some of the dust comes from fires and volcanoes on Earth.

What do we know about Earth's atmosphere? It is made up of layers. Each layer has its own characteristics. The layer closest to the surface of Earth is called the *troposphere* (TRAHP·uh·sfeer). All life on Earth exists here. This is where **weather** (WETH·uhr) takes place. Weather is what the air is like at a given time and place.

▷ **What makes up the atmosphere?**

Layers of the Atmosphere

Thermosphere
The thermosphere is the top layer of the atmosphere. Light displays called the *northern lights* happen here.

Mesosphere
The mesosphere is between the stratosphere and the thermosphere.

Stratosphere
In the stratosphere the air is not still. Very strong winds called the *jet stream* are located here.

Troposphere
The troposphere is the layer of the atmosphere closest to Earth. In this layer clouds, rain, snow, and thunderstorms occur.

READING
Diagrams

1. Which layer is the airplane in?
2. Where does weather take place?

What Is Air Temperature?

What do you say when you go outside on a hot summer day? You say, "It is hot." The *it* is the air.

The Sun heats the air, so it feels hot. It has a high **temperature** (TEM·puhr·uh·chuhr). Temperature is a measure of how hot or cold something is. The Sun also heats Earth's surface—both the land and the water.

Air temperature is always changing. You know that it is usually warmer during the day than at night. The Sun heats Earth and the air.

How can you measure temperature? You need to use a *thermometer*. The diagram at the right shows you how to read a thermometer.

Does all the air around Earth get the same amount of heat from the Sun? Not really. Places near Earth's North and South Poles do not get as much sunlight as places near the equator. The Sun stays low in the sky near the poles. This is one reason why it is warmer near the equator than near the poles.

▶ **What heats the air?**

Measuring Air Temperature

100°C/212°F
Water boils. You can make tea.

30°C/86°F
It's a good day to go to the beach.

10°C/50°F
Wear a jacket.

0°C/32°F
Water freezes. It's cold, so bundle up.

°C °F

READING
Diagrams

1. When would you wear a jacket?
2. At what temperature does water freeze?

What Is Air Pressure?

The weight of the atmosphere presses on you all the time. It presses on everything on Earth. The pressing down force of the air on Earth is called **air pressure**.

Do you feel air pressure? Not usually. Your body is used to air pressure. You don't even notice it most of the time. However, you can notice when air pressure changes. What happens when you climb up a mountain? Your ears "pop." This pop is caused by a change in air pressure pushing on your eardrum. You may also feel your ears pop if you ride in an elevator or fly in an airplane.

▷ **What is air pressure?**

As climbers scale a mountain, the air pressure changes. It decreases. The climbers probably feel their ears "pop."

FOR SCHOOL OR HOME

How Mighty Is the Air?

1. Place a ruler on a desk. Half of the ruler should be hanging off the edge of the desk.

2. Observe Carefully hit the edge of your ruler with your hand. What happens?

3. Cover the ruler with a page of newspaper.

4. Predict What do you think will happen when the ruler is hit? Record your predictions.

5. Observe Hit the ruler again. What happens? Write down your findings.

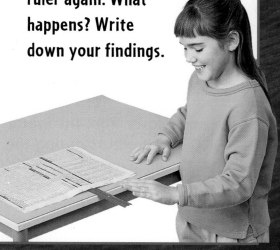

What Happens When Air Moves?

Air moves from an area of high pressure to an area of lower pressure. This moving air is called *wind*.

What if you pour two cups of water toward each other in a sink? What happens when they meet? The water mixes and may even churn and bubble. When two different bodies of air meet, they also mix. Large bodies of air are called air masses. The place where different masses of air meet is where most weather changes happen. Here it may be cloudy or rainy or stormy.

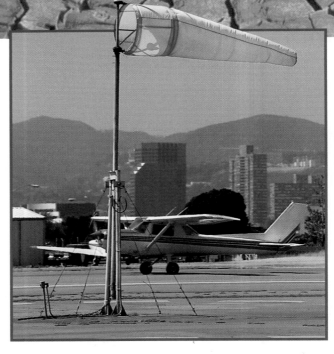

A windsock is a common sight at an airport. It measures the direction of the wind.

READING Summarize
What happens when two different air masses meet?

The Movement of Air

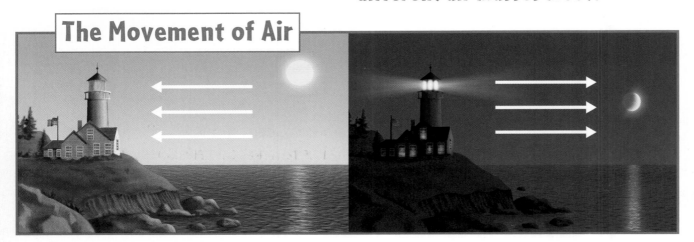

A sea breeze blows from the water onto the shore. It occurs during the day when the air over the water is cooler than the air over the land. Cooler air has higher pressure. Air moves from an area of high pressure to an area of lower pressure.

A land breeze blows from the land onto the water. It occurs during the night when the air over the land is cooler than the air over the water. Cooler air has higher pressure. Air moves from an area of high pressure to an area of lower pressure.

Why It Matters

Weather is the conditions of the atmosphere at a given time and place. Weather is part of your daily life. Weather helps you to decide what to wear, where to go, and even how you feel. Knowing about the conditions of air helps you make better decisions about these things.

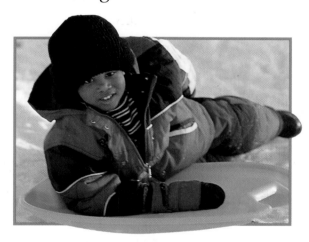

Think and Write

1. Name three properties of weather.

2. What do you use to measure temperature?

3. What is air pressure?

4. What is wind?

5. **Critical Thinking** How can changes in the weather affect your day?

L·I·N·K·S

SOCIAL STUDIES LINK

Use a map. Find Richmond, Virginia, and Wichita, Kansas, on the map. Which city do you think has higher temperatures in winter? In summer? Use the Internet or other resources to get the answers.

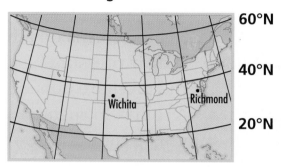

MATH LINK

Make a bar graph. Look at the weather page in a newspaper. Find the average daytime temperature where you live. Record the temperature for seven days. Use the information to make a bar graph. Share it with your teacher.

ART LINK

Create a weather picture. People often say it is raining "cats and dogs" when it is raining very hard. Draw a picture of some strange weather. Write a few sentences to describe your picture.

TECHNOLOGY LINK

At the Computer Visit **www.mhscience02.com** for more links.

Tornadoes
Earth's Great Storm

A thundercloud forms on a hot summer afternoon. The air pressure inside the cloud is lower than the pressure outside. This forces air near the ground to rush into the cloud. The air spins as it moves upward. A tornado is born.

Tornadoes are some of the worst storms on Earth. The winds in a tornado move as fast as 480 kilometers (300 miles) per hour. The tornado acts like a giant vacuum cleaner. It can pick up houses, cars, and anything else in its path.

Most tornadoes are small and don't do much damage. Many of them happen far away from places where people live. A small tornado might last fewer than three minutes. This makes them hard to predict. Only a few tornadoes are large enough to cause much damage. Large tornadoes may last for more than two hours. One giant tornado roared on for seven hours. Their strong winds leave a long path of damage.

The first sign of a tornado is usually a funnel cloud. It extends down from a thundercloud.

How can you protect yourself from tornadoes? When it's stormy outside, check the weather report. A *tornado watch* means that weather conditions could cause a tornado. A *tornado warning* is more serious. This means that a tornado was seen in your area.

The basement is the safest place during a tornado. If you can't go to a basement, go to a closet away from outside walls.

Tornadoes that form over water are called waterspouts.

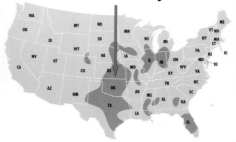

Tornado Alley

More tornadoes occur in the United States than in any other country.

What Did I Learn?

1. What is true about most tornadoes?

  A They are small.
  B They last for three hours.
  C They leave a long path of destruction.
  D They are easy to predict.

2. Where is the safest place when a tornado is near?

  F under a tree
  G in an automobile
  H on the roof
  J in a basement

AT THE COMPUTER

Visit www.mhscience02.com to learn more about tornadoes.

The Water Cycle

Vocabulary

water vapor, D17
evaporation, D17
condensation, D17
water cycle, D18
precipitation, D19

Get Ready

Can you see all of the Golden Gate Bridge? Where do you think the fog that hides it came from? Fog is a cloud that forms near the ground. What are clouds made of?

Process Skill

You make a model when you make something to represent an object or event.

Explore Activity

How Do Raindrops Form?

Materials

clear-plastic jar

plastic wrap

rubber band

marble

ice cubes

warm water

Procedure

1. Fill the jar one-fourth full of warm water.

2. Place plastic wrap over the top of the jar. Use a rubber band to seal the wrap to the jar.

3. Set a marble in the center of the plastic wrap.

4. **Make a Model** Place several small pieces of ice on top of the plastic wrap. You have made a model of Earth. The warm water represents a lake, and the air above it represents the air around Earth.

5. **Observe** Carefully watch the bottom of the plastic wrap.

6. Record your observations.

Drawing Conclusions

1. What did you see inside the jar?

2. Where did the water come from to make the raindrops?

3. **Infer** Do you think water might go into the air faster during the day or the night? Why?

4. **Going Further: Infer** What do you think would have happened if you had poured cold water into the jar instead of warm water?

Main Idea The water cycle is the path water follows on Earth.

Where Does Water Go?

Have you ever seen tiny droplets of water on a bathroom mirror? Where did the droplets come from? Are you surprised to learn that they came from the air?

Everything around you is made up of something called *matter*. Air, water, and this book are all made of matter. Matter can be found in three different forms—solid, liquid, and gas.

A solid is a form of matter that has a definite shape and takes up a definite amount of space. A book is an example of a solid.

A liquid takes up a definite amount of space but does not have a definite shape. A liquid takes the shape of its container. This pitcher of juice is a liquid.

A gas has no definite size or shape. It spreads out to fill the container that holds it. Think of a balloon. The air inside the balloon spreads out to fill the entire balloon.

This journal is a solid.

The juice in this pitcher is a liquid.

Inside this balloon is helium. Helium is a gas.

Water is a type of matter that can be a solid, a liquid, or a gas. How can you change the form of matter?

After it rains, there are puddles in the street. The next day they are gone. Where did the water go? The water went into the air above. When this happens, the water changes. It changes from a liquid into a gas. This gas is **water vapor**. The changing of a liquid into a gas is called **evaporation** (i·vap·uh·RAY·shuhn).

Have you ever seen water droplets on the inside of a window? These water droplets did not come from rain. They came from the air itself! When water vapor in the air cools, it changes back into liquid water. The change of a gas into a liquid is called **condensation** (kahn·den·SAY·shuhn).

Where did this water come from?

READING Summarize

What happens during the process of evaporation?

Where might the water in this lake go?

D 17

What Is the Water Cycle?

Animals and plants use water every day to survive. Where do they get the water they need? They get the water from one or more parts of the **water cycle**. The water cycle is the never-ending path water takes between Earth and the atmosphere.

The Water Cycle

Water condenses
As water vapor rises into the air, it cools. The cooled water vapor changes back into liquid water drops. The liquid water drops form clouds.

Water evaporates
The Sun heats the water in the oceans and on land. The water changes from a liquid into water vapor.

Water evaporates into the air, condenses into clouds, and returns to Earth as **precipitation** (pri·sip·i·TAY·shuhn). Precipitation is water that returns to Earth from the atmosphere. It can be in the form of rain, snow, sleet, or hail.

▶ **What is the water cycle?**

Precipitation

When enough water has condensed in clouds, the water falls to Earth as precipitation. Precipitation can be in the form of rain, snow, sleet, or hail. The form of precipitation depends mainly on the temperature.

Water on the ground

Some precipitation flows downhill into lakes, rivers, and oceans. Some falls directly into these bodies of water. Some precipitation soaks into the ground. This water is called *groundwater*.

READING
Diagrams

1. What part of the water cycle is easy to see?

2. Why is this path of water called a cycle?

Process Skill
BUILDER

How Does Temperature Affect Evaporation?

Does the temperature of the air affect evaporation? How could you find out? In this activity you will make a model and then infer to investigate this question.

Materials

water

2 plastic cups

marker

Procedure

1 **Make a Model** Fill each cup half full with water. Use the marker to show where the water level is.

2 Place one cup in a warm place. Place the other cup in a cool place.

3 **Predict** In which cup will the water level change the most? Record your prediction.

4 **Observe** Look at the cups every day for one week. How did the amount of water change? Write down what happened.

Drawing Conclusions

1 **Infer** Where did the water in each cup go?

2 How did the amount of water differ after two days?

3 How does this compare with your prediction?

4 **Infer** How could you use this model to make seawater drinkable?

Why It Matters

Water is one of our most important resources. You need to drink fresh water every day. Plants and animals need water, too. The water cycle is nature's way of recycling. The continuous movement of water through the water cycle provides us with fresh, clean water.

Think and Write

1. What is water vapor?

2. Why does a puddle seem to disappear?

3. What determines whether precipitation is rain or snow?

4. **Make a Model** Draw a picture to show evaporation and condensation.

5. **Critical Thinking** What do you think might happen if there were no water cycle?

L·I·N·K·S

MATH LINK

Solve a problem. Ten inches of snow is approximately equal to one inch of rain. If it snowed five inches, how much rain would that be?

ART LINK

Create a poster. Make a list of the different ways you can use water. Then find or draw pictures of these ways. Use them to make a poster.

WRITING LINK

Write a poem. Write the words *water cycle* down the side of a sheet of paper. Think of words that describe the water cycle, and start with each letter in the two words. Arrange these words in a poem.

TECHNOLOGY LINK

At the Computer Visit **www.mhscience02.com** for more links.

Describing Weather

Get Ready

Look outside. Is it sunny? Is it raining? When you were outside, how did it feel? What is the weather like where you live? How do you measure the conditions of the air? For example, how can you measure air temperature?

Process Skill

You measure when you find the temperature and air pressure.

Explore Activity

How Do You Measure Temperature?

Procedure

1 Predict Where do you think the air temperature in your classroom is the highest and the lowest? Record your predictions.

2 Measure Use a thermometer to find the air temperature at several places in the classroom. Also hold the thermometer outside for two minutes. Then read and record the temperature. Remember to include the places in your predictions.

3 How did your measurements compare with your predictions?

Drawing Conclusions

1 What was the warmest spot in your classroom? What was the coolest spot in your classroom?

2 Communicate Use the measurements to make a bar graph.

3 Going Further: Predict What if you were doing this activity in the playground? Predict where you think the air temperature would be the highest and the lowest. Would it be better to make measurements on a calm or windy day? Why?

Main Idea Temperature, air pressure, and wind speed can be measured.

How Do You Describe Weather?

When scientists describe weather, they measure temperature, air pressure, and amount of precipitation. They also measure the speed and direction of the wind.

You measure the temperature of the air with a thermometer. These pictures show the main weather instruments and what they measure.

A **thermometer** (thuhr·MAHM·i·tuhr) measures the temperature of the air. Indoor-outdoor thermometers give the air temperature both inside the house and outside at the same time.

A *rain gauge* measures how much precipitation has fallen.

A **barometer** (buh·RAHM·i·tuhr) measures air pressure. If the reading on the barometer is rising, it usually means fair weather is coming. A falling barometer reading usually means precipitation is on its way.

READING **Summarize**
What instruments do you use to describe weather?

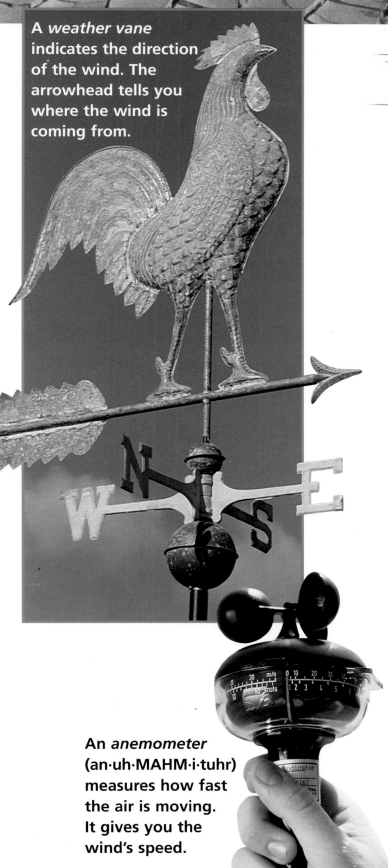

A *weather vane* indicates the direction of the wind. The arrowhead tells you where the wind is coming from.

An *anemometer* (an·uh·MAHM·i·tuhr) measures how fast the air is moving. It gives you the wind's speed.

QUICK LAB

Make a Barometer

1. Firmly place four paper clips on the rim of a plastic cup. Space them equally around.

2. Fill the cup two-thirds full of water. Place a bowl over the cup as shown.

3. Turn the bowl and the cup of water over.

4. Mark the level of the water in the cup. Set the bowl outside.

5. **Observe** Watch the water level for five days. Record your observations.

6. **Infer** Was your barometer able to predict the weather? Explain your answer.

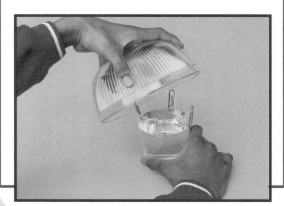

D 25

How Do You Read a Weather Map?

What do you do when you make observations? You write them down. You might also share your data with other people.

Scientists gather data about the weather. They use symbols to show the data on a large weather map. The map shows weather conditions over a large area. Scientists then share this information with others and make weather forecasts.

Look at the weather map of the United States below. This weather map shows you cloud cover, temperature, and other current weather conditions. Some places, such as Phoenix, are having hot, sunny weather. Other places, such as New York City, are cooler and rainy. Each color band represents an area where the temperature falls in the same range.

▷ **What does a weather map show?**

READING

Maps

1. What is the predicted temperature for Phoenix, Arizona?

2. What is the predicted cloud cover for Atlanta, Georgia?

Reading a Weather Map

CANADA

Portland · Butte

San Francisco · 70s 60s

80s Denver

90s

100s

Phoenix · 80s

Dallas

MEXICO

Chicago · 70s 80s

80s

90s

New York City

Richmond

70s

Atlanta

90s

60s

KEY

❄	Flurries
❄❄	Snow
🌢	Ice
🌧	Rain
⚡	Thunder
☀	Sunny
☁	Cloudy
⛅	Partly cloudy

Why It Matters

Listening to a weather report can help you answer questions. What should I wear today? Will I go hiking tomorrow? Being able to read a weather map yourself is really awesome! For example, if you see that cities west of you are having rain, you'll probably have rain the next day.

Visit www.mhscience02.com to do a research project on the weather.

Think and Write

1. How do you measure temperature?

2. What does a barometer measure?

3. Name two other weather instruments. What do they measure?

4. What information does a weather map provide?

5. Critical Thinking How might you use the information from a weather report?

L·I·N·K·S

LITERATURE LINK

Read *Stormy Weather* to learn about the weather. When you finish reading, list some of the kinds of weather in the story. Try the activities at the end of the book.

SOCIAL STUDIES LINK

Do research. This weather-satellite photo shows a hurricane heading for Florida. Some areas of the United States have more hurricanes than others. Do research to find out which U.S. regions have the most hurricanes. Can you explain why?

ART LINK

Make a cloud poster. Observe the clouds in the sky. Record your observations. Then use cotton balls to model some of the clouds you have seen.

TECHNOLOGY LINK

At the Computer Visit www.mhscience02.com for more links.

The Ups and Downs of Tides

If you live near the ocean, you probably know about tides. Tides are the rise and fall of the ocean's water level. Places along the ocean's shore usually have two high tides each day. The water level is high, and the edge of the ocean moves inland. In between high tides are low tides. The water level is low, and the edge of the ocean moves back out.

What causes tides? The answer comes from outer space! The Moon's gravity causes the oceans to bulge in some places and shrink in others. Because the Moon and Earth are always moving, tides rise and fall every day. Gravity from the Sun also affects tides.

At some places along the shore, you can find tide pools. Tide pools are puddles of water that a high tide leaves behind. It's fun to explore tide pools. You might find sea stars, crabs, or other sea creatures.

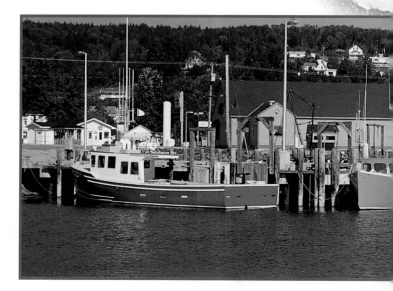

It is high tide. The water level is high.

It is low tide. Look at what happened to the water level.

People can find shells and interesting sea creatures in tide pools.

Write ABOUT IT

1. What causes tides to rise and fall?
2. How might tides affect the lives of people who live by the ocean?

AT THE COMPUTER

Visit www.mhscience02.com to learn more about tides.

Chapter 7 Review

Vocabulary

Fill each blank with the best word or words from the list.

air pressure, D9   **precipitation,** D17
atmosphere, D6   **temperature,** D8
barometer, D24   **thermometer,** D24
condensation,   **water vapor,** D17
   D17   **weather,** D6
evaporation, D17

1. The air around Earth is a mixture of gases and dust called the _____.

2. The _____ of something measures how hot or cold it is.

3. The force of air pushing down on Earth is called _____.

4. Water in a gas form is called _____.

5. Rain, snow, hail, and sleet fall to Earth and are called _____.

6. A tool used to measure air pressure is a(n) _____.

7. The condition of the atmosphere at a given time and place is the _____.

8. To measure air temperature, you would use a(n) _____.

The water cycle is a never-ending process of precipitation,

9. _____

10. _____.

Test Prep

11. In which layer of the atmosphere does all weather take place?

    A troposphere

    B stratosphere

    C ozone

    D outer space

12. The change from a gas into a liquid is _____.

    F evaporation

    G condensation

    H precipitation

    J runoff

13. A weather map shows _____.

    A temperature ranges

    B cloud cover

    C precipitation

    D all of the above

14. A weather vane is used to measure _____.

    F wind

    G rainfall

    H temperature

    J air pressure

15. After it rains, some water soaks into the ground to become _____.

    A water vapor

    B ground water

    C runoff

    D precipitation

Concepts and Skills

16. **Reading in Science** Study the drawing. Describe how water moves through the water cycle. Use the words *evaporation*, *condensation*, and *precipitation* in your answer.

17. **Critical Thinking** Air pressure is much lower on mountains than it is in valleys. Why do you think this is so?

18. **Process Skills: Infer** If you pour lemonade into a cold glass, drops of water form outside the glass. What causes the drops to form?

19. **Scientific Methods** For the past two weeks, what was the average temperature in your town? Use newspapers or the Internet to answer this question.

20. **Decision Making** Pretend you're a farmer. Fall has arrived and you need to harvest your crops. How does the weather affect you? What decisions might you make based on the weather?

Earth in Space

Did You Ever Wonder?

How do scientists learn about space? One way is to look at the night sky through a telescope. Powerful telescopes are often put in buildings called observatories. Observatories are built on mountains or hilltops, away from the lights of cities. What do we know about the objects in space?

How Earth Moves

Vocabulary

sphere, D36

rotate, D36

axis, D37

revolve, D38

orbit, D38

Get Ready

Have you ever watched the Sun set and turn day into night? Have you watched the Sun rise? A dark sky brightens with just a peek of the Sun. What do you think causes night and day?

Process Skill

You make a model when you make something to represent an object or event.

Explore Activity

What Causes Day and Night?

Materials

globe

medium self-stick notes

flashlight

Procedure

1. Write *I live here* on a self-stick note. Place the note over the United States on the globe.

2. While one person holds the globe, shine the flashlight on the self-stick note.

3. **Observe** If the flashlight is the Sun, would it be day or night on the self-stick note? Is it day or night on the other side of the globe? Record your observations.

4. Think of two different ways to make it night at the place near the self-stick note. Record your ideas.

5. **Make a Model** Use the globe and the flashlight to test your ideas.

Drawing Conclusions

1. How did you create day and night in the first model and in the second model?

2. Which idea do you think better explains what you know about day and night? Why?

3. **Going Further: Infer** You put your wet sneakers in sunlight to dry. An hour later they are in shade. Explain what happened.

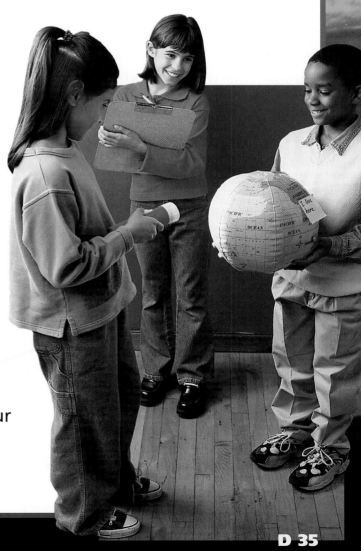

Main Idea Earth's rotation causes day and night, and its revolution causes the seasons.

What Causes Day and Night?

A long time ago, people thought that Earth stood still while the Sun traveled around it each day. It's easy to see why people once thought the Sun moved. Every day we see the Sun seem to come up, move across the sky, and go down. Today we know that the Sun does not move around Earth.

It is the movement of Earth that causes day and night. Earth is shaped like a ball. This shape is called a **sphere** (SFEER). Earth **rotates** (ROH·taytz). To rotate means to turn. As Earth rotates, there is daylight where Earth faces the Sun and darkness where Earth is turned away from the Sun.

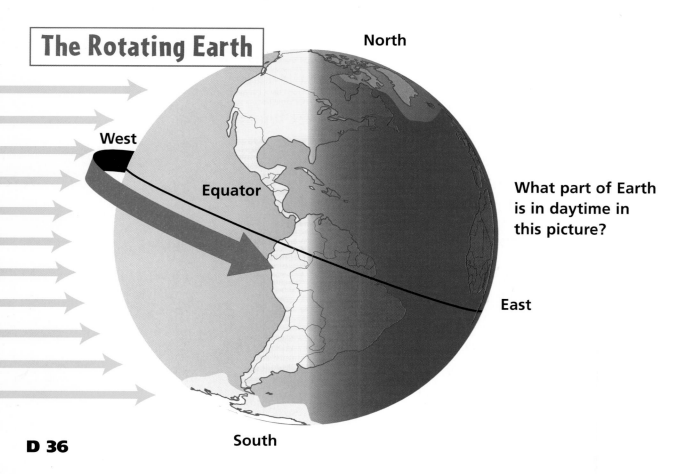

The Rotating Earth

North

West

Equator

What part of Earth is in daytime in this picture?

East

South

It takes 24 hours for Earth to make one complete rotation. One complete rotation is one day. A day is made up of the hours of light and the hours of dark.

Look at the illustration below. Notice the line drawn through the center of Earth. This imaginary line is called an **axis** (AK·sis). Earth spins, or rotates, around its axis. As you can see, Earth's axis is not straight up and down. It is slightly tilted. At the north end of Earth's axis is the North Pole. At the south end is the South Pole.

The tilt of Earth changes how the Sun's rays strike the surface. At the poles the Sun stays low in the sky during the day. Here the Sun's rays are weak. This is why it is cold at the poles. At the equator the Sun rises high in the sky during the day. These rays are stronger. Here the air temperature is higher.

What is an axis?

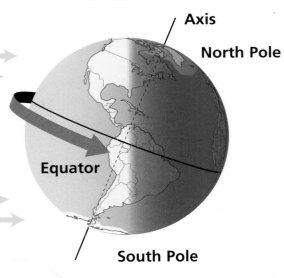

Axis

North Pole

Equator

South Pole

This tortoise lives near the equator. The temperature is warmer here.

These penguins live near the South Pole. The temperature is colder here.

What Causes the Seasons?

Rotation is only one way in which Earth moves. Earth also **revolves** (ri·VAHLVZ). An object that moves around another object revolves. Earth travels in a regular path around the Sun. It travels in an **orbit** (AWR·bit). An orbit is the path that an object follows as it revolves around another object. It takes one year, or $365\frac{1}{4}$ days, for Earth to make one complete revolution around the Sun.

In many parts of the world, the year is made up of four seasons—winter, spring, summer, and fall. Why do we have seasons? The answer has to do with Earth's tilted axis. Having a tilted axis means that Earth slants a little as it revolves around the Sun.

Look at the diagram. Notice that Earth is always tilted in the same direction. As Earth travels around the Sun, the part of Earth tilted toward the Sun changes. For part of the year, the North Pole tilts toward the Sun. During another part of the year, the North Pole tilts away from the Sun.

Summer
(begins June 21–22)
North America is tilted toward the Sun. The Sun is higher overhead, and the temperature is warmer.

READING
Diagrams

If it is summer in the northern half of Earth, what season is it in the southern half?

When the North Pole is tilted toward the Sun, the Sun travels higher overhead in the sky. The Sun's rays shine straighter down on that part of Earth. It is then summer in that part of Earth. When the North Pole is tilted away from the Sun, the Sun stays lower in the sky. It is then winter in that part of Earth.

Earth Revolves Around the Sun

▷ What is a year?

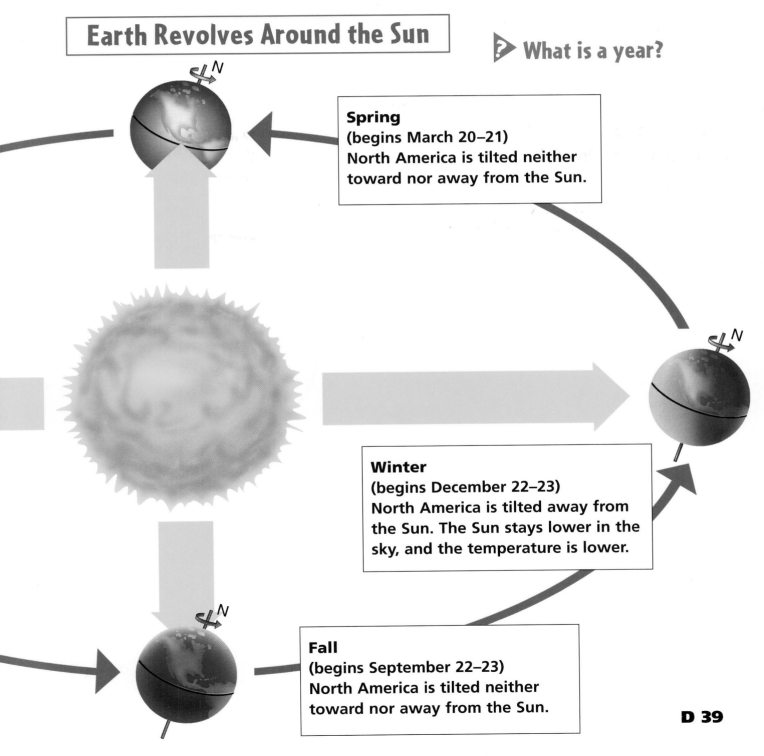

Spring
(begins March 20–21)
North America is tilted neither toward nor away from the Sun.

Winter
(begins December 22–23)
North America is tilted away from the Sun. The Sun stays lower in the sky, and the temperature is lower.

Fall
(begins September 22–23)
North America is tilted neither toward nor away from the Sun.

QUICK LAB

FOR SCHOOL OR HOME

Sundial

1. Tape a piece of paper to some cardboard. Use clay to anchor a pencil straight up at the center of the paper.

2. Take your sundial outside on a sunny morning.

3. **Measure** Use a marker to draw a line through the middle of the pencil's shadow. Label the line with the time of day. Measure and mark the pencil's shadow again at 12 noon and 3 P.M.

4. Repeat step 3 once a month.

5. How does the shadow's position change in one day? Is the Sun high or low in the sky when the shadows are the longest?

6. **Infer** During which month is the Sun's path highest in the sky? Lowest?

How Does the Sun's Path in the Sky Change?

As the seasons change, so does the way the Sun appears to travel across the sky each day. In summer your part of Earth is tilted toward the Sun. The Sun's path appears higher in the sky. In winter your part of Earth is tilted away from the Sun. The Sun's path appears lower in the sky.

READING **Cause and Effect**
What causes the Sun to appear higher in the sky during the summer?

The Sun in the Summer and Winter Skies

June

December

Set

Rise

Why It Matters

The way Earth moves affects the way we lead our lives. Just think of all the things you do during the day and those you do at night. Also think about what you do throughout the year. Do you have a favorite season? Do you enjoy hot summer days, or do you like cooler ones? How about riding a sled down a snowy hill? What do you like to do when it rains or snows?

Think and Write

1. If it is nighttime at a certain place on Earth, is that place facing toward or away from the Sun?

2. Describe the motion of Earth that makes up one day.

3. How are rotating and revolving different?

4. What would happen to the seasons if Earth's axis were not tilted?

5. **Critical Thinking** How would your life be different if you lived in the southern half of Earth?

L·I·N·K·S

MATH LINK

Solve a problem. It would take you about 3 months to walk around the Moon and about 11 months to walk around Earth. How many months would it take to walk around both? Would that time be more than a year or less than a year?

HEALTH LINK

Conduct an interview. Ultraviolet (ul·truh·VIGH·uh·lit) light (UV) from the Sun causes a suntan or sunburn. Interview adult family members to find out how they protect their skin. Write down what they tell you.

WRITING LINK

Write a story. Describe how your life would change if Earth made one complete rotation every 12 hours. Share your story.

TECHNOLOGY LINK

Science Newsroom CD-ROM Choose *Around the World* to learn how Earth's position affects seasons.

At the Computer Visit **www.mhscience02.com** for more links.

Star Time

Could you tell time without a clock or calendar? Ancient people had to, because there were no clocks or calendars!

Ancient farmers needed to keep track of time. They had to know when to plant their crops. Their lives depended on planting at the right time to get the food they needed. How did they do it? They used the stars!

The farmers carefully studied the skies. They noticed that groups of stars formed shapes, or constellations. They saw that different constellations were visible at different times of the year. For thousands of years, people used constellations to predict the seasons.

Orion, the hunter, is a constellation. Let's say that it's winter in the Northern Hemisphere, and you study the night sky. If you observe Orion every night, at the same time, from the same spot—like your bedroom window—you'll notice that Orion seems to move across the sky! What's really happening? Earth is rotating and revolving around the Sun, so you're the one who's moving past Orion!

In spring, Orion starts to disappear from the night sky. Perhaps ancient farmers used this as a sign to start planting their crops. As winter

What Did I Learn?

1. What did ancient farmers use to tell time?

   A   roman numerals
   B   stars
   C   rocks
   D   They didn't need to tell time.

2. Pick the best definition of the word *constellation*.

   F   Orion, the hunter
   G   ancient farmer
   H   group of stars
   J   calendar

AT THE COMPUTER

Visit www.mhscience02.com to learn more about the seasons.

Phases of the Moon

Get Ready

Have you ever seen the Moon when it looked like this? Although the Moon is in the sky each day, it doesn't always look the same. Sometimes it is a full circle, and sometimes it is a thin slice. Why does the Moon seem to change shape?

Process Skill

You **communicate** when you share information.

Explore Activity

Materials

lamp

volleyball

Why Does the Moon's Shape Change?

Procedure

1 **Observe** From your seat, look at the ball closely. Draw the ball.

2 **Make a Model** Turn off the classroom lights. Turn on the lamp, and shine it on one side of the ball. Draw the shape of the ball where the light hits it.

3 **Infer** Compare all the drawings. What do you think caused the different shapes?

Drawing Conclusions

1 How did the ball look when you first observed it? How did it look in the darkened room?

2 Why did your classmates see different lighted shapes?

3 **Infer** In this model the ball is the Moon and the lamp is the Sun. What are you?

4 **Going Further: Infer** Why does the Moon appear to change its shape?

How Does the Moon's Shape Change?

Night after night the Moon seems to change shape. Sometimes you can see only a small part of the Moon. Other times it is a big, bright circle. Still other times you can't see it at all. The Moon is a **satellite** (SAT·uh·light) of Earth. A satellite is anything that orbits another larger object in space. Half of the Moon always faces toward the Sun. The other half always faces away from the Sun.

The Moon, like a ball, is a sphere. The Moon does not change shape. It only appears to change shape because you see different amounts of its lighted part as it orbits Earth. The positions of the Sun and the Moon make it seem to change shape.

As the Moon orbits Earth, our view of it changes. The Moon appears to have different shapes. These changing shapes are called the Moon's **phases** (FAYZ·uhz). It takes about 29 days for the Moon to pass through all of its phases. Then the phases repeat. The four main phases of the Moon are new Moon, first quarter, full Moon, and last quarter.

The harvest Moon rises around sunset. This Moon got its name because it provided extra light for farmers in the north to harvest their crops.

▷ **Why does the Moon appear to change shape?**

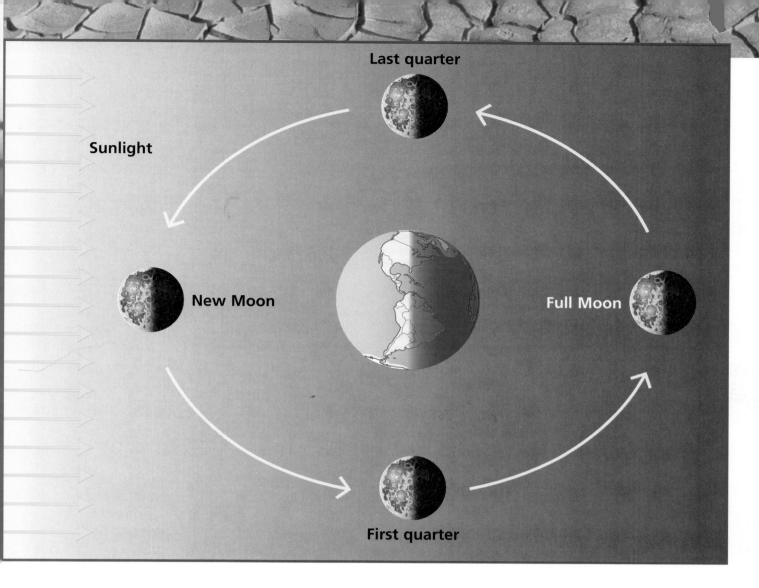

Last quarter

Sunlight

New Moon

Full Moon

First quarter

① New Moon   ② First quarter   ③ Full Moon   ④ Last quarter

READING

Diagrams

List four phases of the Moon.

As the Moon orbits Earth, one side is always lighted. As the Moon changes position, different parts of its lighted side are seen from Earth. No matter what shape it may look like, the Moon is always a sphere.

The U.S. *Apollo 11* astronauts landed on the Moon on July 20, 1969.

How Are Earth and the Moon Different?

Both Earth and the Moon are spheres that rotate and revolve. They also receive light from the Sun. In most ways, however, Earth and the Moon are quite different. A day on Earth lasts 24 hours, while a day on the Moon lasts more than 27 Earth days.

The Moon is about one-fourth the size of Earth. The Moon has less mass than Earth. The Moon also has less gravity. The Moon's gravity is about one-sixth of Earth's gravity. If you weigh 30 kilograms (66 pounds) on Earth, you would weigh only 5 kilograms (11 pounds) on the Moon!

Craters (KRAY·tuhrz) cover most of the Moon's surface. A crater is a hollow area, or pit, in the ground. Some of the Moon's craters may have been formed by ancient volcanoes. Most, however, were caused by chunks of rock or metal from space that crashed into the Moon. Some of the Moon's craters are very large. Others are quite small.

Earth has few craters. Most objects from space burn up before they reach Earth. The air and water on Earth also cause craters here to erode, or wear away. The Moon has no air.

Water is found in many places on Earth. It is in the air. It is in oceans, rivers, lakes, and streams. Water is also found in the ground. The Moon has no liquid water. Water is needed by all living things. Because the Moon has no air or liquid water, there can be no life there. Astronauts were able to visit the Moon because their spacesuits provided air and protection from the heat.

READING **Cause and Effect**
What causes the craters on the Moon's surface?

Earth's surface is almost three-quarters water. There are few craters on Earth. Earth supports life.

Large and small craters cover the Moon's rocky surface. There is no liquid water on the Moon.

D 49

Process Skill BUILDER

SKILL Predict

Use Patterns

Rachel observed the Moon on different days during one month. She drew her observations on this calendar. There were some days she did not observe the Moon. Can you predict the shape of the Moon on the days she did not observe it?

Procedure

1 **Observe** Study the calendar shown here.

2 Look for similar shapes and patterns of the Moon.

Drawing Conclusions

1 **Predict** What do you think the Moon's shape was on Wednesday, January 9? Compare it with the shape of the Moon on January 8 and January 11. Draw your prediction.

2 **Predict** What was the Moon's shape on Friday, January 25? Compare it with the shape of the Moon on January 24 and January 26. Draw your prediction.

3 **Predict** Draw the shape of the Moon you would expect to see on January 29. What helped you decide on that shape?

4 **Communicate** What helps you predict Moon shapes? What do you need to know to predict the shape of tomorrow's Moon?

JANUARY						
Sunday	Monday	Tuesday	Wednesday	Thursday	Friday	Saturday
		1	2	3	4	5
6	7	8	9	10	11	12
13	14	15	16	17	18	19
20	21	22	23	24	25	26
27	28	29	30	31		

D 50

L·I·N·K·S

Why It Matters

Earth provides you with things you need to survive, such as water, air, and temperatures that aren't too hot or too cold. The Moon is Earth's nearest neighbor in space. However, the Moon cannot support life. It is very hot in some places and very cold in others. The Moon doesn't have any air or liquid water.

Think and Write

1. What shape is the Moon? Why does it appear to change shape?

2. Explain what the term "a phase of the Moon" means. Identify the four main phases.

3. Why does the Moon appear to shine?

4. **Predict** Last night it was a new Moon. What will the next main phase be?

5. **Critical Thinking** Why is there no life on the Moon?

MATH LINK

What's your Moon weight? How much would you weigh on the Moon? It's easy to figure out. Weigh yourself at home. Your weight will probably be in pounds. Divide your Earth weight by six to find your Moon weight. Use a calculator to help you.

LITERATURE LINK

Read *Up, Up, and Away!* to learn about Mae Jemison, the first African American woman to go into space. When you finish reading this book, imagine a day on the space shuttle. Try the activities at the end of the book.

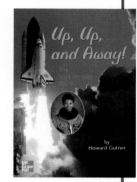

WRITING LINK

Write a story. Describe what you think it would be like to live on the Moon. What things would you need that the Moon does not provide? How would you get those things? Include drawings along with your story.

TECHNOLOGY LINK

At the Computer Visit **www.mhscience02.com** for more links.

The Sun and Its Planets

Get Ready

When you look at the night sky, you see many different objects. You can see the Moon and the stars. You can also see some of Earth's other neighbors—planets. What do you see when you look up at the night sky?

Process Skill

You observe when you use one or more of the senses to identify or learn about an object or event.

Explore Activity

How Do Planets Move?

Materials

sign for each planet

2 signs for the Sun

Procedure

1 Make a Model Take turns with other groups of classmates. Model the motion of the planets around the Sun. When you are not doing the modeling, make as many observations as you can.

2 Observe Listen to the student who is modeling Earth. He or she will describe what can be seen from Earth in the night sky.

Drawing Conclusions

1 What planets were visible from Earth the first time you modeled the motions of the planets? What planets were visible the second time?

2 How did Earth's motion affect what planets could be seen from Earth? How did the motion of the other planets affect what planets could be seen from Earth?

3 Why does the position of the planets in the night sky change?

4 Going Further: Predict What would have happened if you had moved faster around the Sun? If you had moved slower?

Read to Learn

Main Idea Our solar system includes the
Sun, the nine planets, and their moons.

What Is the Solar System?

The Sun, Earth, and the Moon are part of a larger
system called the **solar system**. The solar system is
made up of the Sun and all the objects that orbit it.

Earth is one of nine **planets** (PLAN·itz) that orbit the
Sun. A planet is a large body of rock or gas that orbits
the Sun. Each planet is a different size. Some are smaller
than Earth, and some are larger. Each planet rotates on
its axis and revolves around the Sun as Earth does. Here
is the order of the planets from the Sun: Mercury, Venus,
Earth, Mars, Jupiter, Saturn, Uranus, Neptune, and
Pluto. This sentence may help you remember the order:
My Very Excellent Mother Just Served Us Nine Pizzas.

The Nine Planets Revolve Around the Sun

Sun

Mercury

Venus

Earth

Mars

The Sun is a **star**. A star is a hot, glowing ball of gases. The Sun is only a medium-sized star. It looks larger than any other star because it is the closest star to Earth.

The Sun is very big compared with Earth. It is so big that if it were hollow, more than one million Earths would fit inside it! The Sun looks small because it is very far from Earth. The Sun is so far away that it takes eight minutes for sunlight to make the trip to Earth.

Earth gets heat as well as light from the Sun. It's a good thing we live at this distance from the Sun. If we were much closer, Earth would be too hot to live on. If we were much farther away, Earth would be too cold for living things.

▷ **What is in our solar system?**

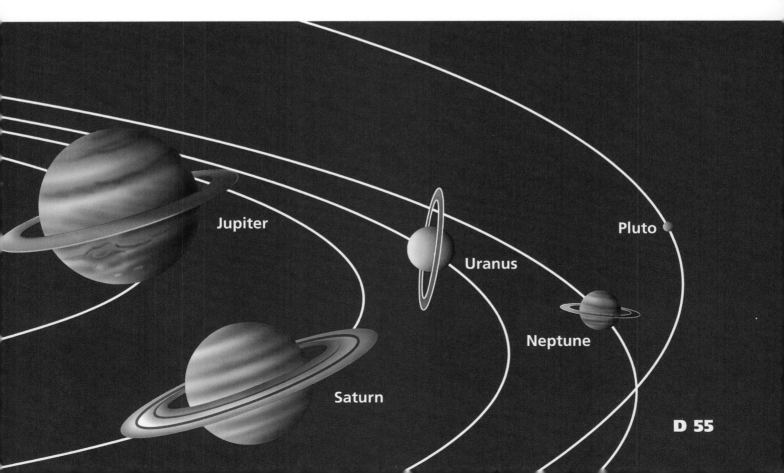

Jupiter

Uranus

Pluto

Neptune

Saturn

Mercury is the closest planet to the Sun. It looks a lot like Earth's Moon.

What Are the Nine Planets Like?

Like the Moon, planets have no light of their own. They reflect sunlight. Light reflected from the surface of the Moon and the planets shines steadily.

The name *planet* comes from a word meaning "wanderer." True to their name, planets appear to wander through the sky. Each planet moves in a different orbit and at a different speed. The planets are always moving and changing positions.

The planets are divided into two groups—the inner planets and the outer planets. The inner planets are the four planets closest to the Sun—Mercury, Venus, Earth, and Mars.

The inner planets are all small and made up of solid, rocklike materials.

Space probes have visited cloud-covered **Venus** many times.

Mars has some water, but most of it is frozen ice. Mars is known as the "red planet" because of its reddish rocks and soil.

Earth is our home. It is the only planet with liquid water.

Jupiter is the largest planet in our solar system. The Great Red Spot on Jupiter has been whirling around for 300 years.

Saturn is known for its thousands of beautiful rings. They are made up of different-sized bits of ice and rock that orbit the planet.

The outer planets are Jupiter, Saturn, Uranus, Neptune, and Pluto. All of the outer planets are made up mostly of gases, except for Pluto. Pluto is made up of a mixture of rocky materials and frozen gases. The outer planets are much colder than the inner planets. They are farther from the Sun.

READING **Cause and Effect**

What causes the outer planets to be colder than the inner planets?

Uranus is called the "sideways planet" because it rotates on its side.

Neptune is more than two billion miles from Earth. It has a Great Dark Spot similar to Jupiter's Great Red Spot.

Little is known about **Pluto** because it is so far away.

QUICK LAB

Make a Letter Larger

1. Cover a piece of newspaper with some wax paper.

2. **Observe** Put a small drop of water over a letter. How does it look?

3. **Experiment** Put water drops of different sizes over other letters. Observe.

4. How does the size of the drop affect the way the print looks?

5. **Infer** How is the curved lens in a telescope like the drop of water?

The objects in our solar system are easier to see with a telescope.

How Do We Learn About Space?

The Sun, the Moon, and the planets are very far away. How do scientists learn about them? One tool they use is a **telescope** (TEL·uh·skohp). A telescope gathers light to make faraway objects appear larger, closer, and clearer. Telescopes gather light with mirrors and **lenses** (LENZ·uhz). A lens is a curved piece of glass.

▷ **What does a telescope do?**

Lesson Review

Why It Matters

The solar system is Earth's "family" in space. Since early times people have wanted to know more about the other planets. Today telescopes and space probes give us a lot of important information. Do you like to look at the stars and planets at night? Now you know how to tell which objects are planets!

Visit **www.mhscience02.com** to do a research project on the solar system.

Think and Write

1. What is the solar system?

2. What two things does Earth receive from the Sun?

3. Name the four inner planets. Choose one, and describe its features.

4. How would life be different without the telescope?

5. **Critical Thinking** What if the outer planets were farther away from the Sun? How would this affect the planets' orbits around the Sun?

L·I·N·K·S

WRITING LINK

Write a story. Imagine yourself on a trip through space. What tools have you taken with you? What do you see as you pass by Mercury, Venus, Earth, and Mars?

SOCIAL STUDIES LINK

Use research materials. Research the history of space exploration. Write down your findings. Share the information with your classmates.

LITERATURE LINK

Read *Mars Discovery* to learn about Mars. When you finish reading, make a list of the ways that Earth is similar to Mars. Try the activities at the end of the book.

TECHNOLOGY LINK

Science Newsroom CD-ROM Choose *Out for a Spin* to learn how Earth and Mars rotate and revolve.

At the Computer Visit **www.mhscience02.com** for more links.

Chapter 8 Review

Vocabulary

Fill in each blank with the best word from the list.

axis, D37   **revolve,** D38
crater, D49   **rotate,** D36
orbit, D38   **satellite,** D46
phase, D46   **star,** D55
planet, D54   **telescope,** D58

1. Earth revolves or travels in a(n) _____ around the Sun.

2. A new Moon and a full Moon are two of the Moon's _____.

3. Mercury, Mars, and Earth are three of nine _____ in our solar system.

4. A tool that makes faraway objects seem closer is a(n) _____.

5. Anything that orbits another larger object in space is a(n) _____.

6. When a meteorite slams into the Moon, it makes a hollow area called a(n) _____.

7. Earth spins on an imaginary line called a(n) _____.

8. The Sun is a medium-sized _____.

Two ways Earth moves are that it:

9. _____

10. _____.

Test Prep

11. There are days and nights because _____.

   A the Sun rotates

   B the Moon rotates

   C Earth rotates

   D the Moon revolves around the Sun

12. Earth revolves around _____.

   F the equator

   G the poles

   H the Moon

   J the Sun

13. The apparent changes in the Moon's shape are the Moon's _____.

   A craters

   B phases

   C orbits

   D seasons

14. The two planets closest to Earth are _____.

    F Mars and Venus

    G Mars and Jupiter

    H Mars and the Moon

    J Venus and Mercury

15. The largest planet is _____.

    A Earth

    B Saturn

    C Jupiter

    D Mars

Concepts and Skills

16. Reading in Science Why does the Moon appear to change shape when viewed from Earth? Use the diagram below to help you answer the question.

17. Critical Thinking Some places on Earth have 24 hours of daylight in the summer and 24 hours of darkness in the winter. Where are these places? Explain your answer.

18. Process Skills: Predict How would Earth's weather be different if Earth's axis was straight up and down, instead of tilted?

19. Product Ads Find ads or labels for suntan lotion or sunscreen. Explain what the products claim to do. How do the ads or labels try to interest people in the product?

20. Scientific Methods Scientists use tools to help them observe things. What tool discussed in this chapter has helped scientists to understand planets? How has it helped?

Boost *your test scores!*

Be Smart!
Visit www.mhscience02.com to learn more.

Dr. Jill Tarter
Astronomer

Have you ever looked up at the stars and wondered if there's life up there? Dr. Jill Tarter wonders about that, too. She's trying to find life in space.

Dr. Tarter is an astronomer for SETI. SETI is a group of scientists who search for life in outer space. One way they search is to listen to sounds from space. They hope that one day the sounds will be from other beings. They call these beings extraterrestrials, or ETs.

Dr. Tarter and her team use special telescopes to listen to about 1,000 nearby stars for signals. One day the SETI scientists thought they heard a signal. This was important to SETI astronomers. It meant it might be from an ET. The team was very excited. As they listened more closely, they discovered it was a false alarm. The signal was coming from Earth.

Dr. Tarter knows we may not be able to contact life in space. It is a very big universe. If there is life, it is very far away. She also knows how important it would be to hear just one signal. It would mean we are not alone in the universe.

Dr. Jill Tarter

NATIONAL
GEOGRAPHIC

Write ABOUT IT

1. Describe the job of a SETI scientist.
2. How do you think you'd feel if you found out there was life on other planets?

Careers IN SCIENCE

Here are some different types of careers related to the study of astronomy. You can use the Internet or library resources to find out more about these careers.

- planetarium lecturer
- astronaut
- meteorologist
- physicist

Dr. Tarter with her team of SETI (Search for Extraterrestrial Intelligence) scientists

AT THE COMPUTER

Visit **www.mhscience02.com** to learn more about careers.

WATER CYCLE Story

Your goal is to write a story about the water cycle.

What to Do

Imagine you are a drop of water in a lake. What happens to you as you pass through each phase of the water cycle? How would you feel? Write a story about your adventures as a water drop. Your story should explain the water cycle.

Illustrate your pages with pictures and diagrams.

Moon-Phase Flip Book

Your goal is to make a flip book that shows the phases of the Moon.

What to Do

Draw pictures of the Moon's phases in the small squares. Draw the new Moon, the full Moon, and the stages in between. Cut out your pictures. Put the pictures in order beginning with the new Moon. Staple the pictures together.

Draw Conclusions

How many days does it take for the Moon to pass through all its phases? Are the Moon's phases caused by Earth's shadow on the Moon?

For Your Reference

Science Handbook

Health Handbook

Glossary

Index

Units of Measurement

Temperature

1. The temperature is 77 degrees Fahrenheit.

2. That is the same as 25 degrees Celsius.

3. Water boils at 212 degrees Fahrenheit.

4. Water freezes at 0 degrees Celsius.

Length and Area

1. This classroom is 10 meters wide and 20 meters long.

2. That means the area is 200 square meters.

2. 32 ounces is the same as 2 pounds.

3. The mass of the bat is 907 grams.

Mass and Weight

1. That baseball bat weighs 32 ounces.

Measurement

Volume of Fluids

Rate

Weight/Force

1. This bottle of juice has a volume of 1 liter.

2. That is a little more than 1 quart.

3. I weigh 85 pounds. That is a force of 380.8 newtons.

1. She can walk 20 meters in 5 seconds.

2. That means her speed is 4 meters per second.

Table of Measurements

SI (International System) of Units	English System of Units
Temperature Water freezes at 0 degrees Celsius (°C) and boils at 100°C.	**Temperature** Water freezes at 32 degrees Fahrenheit (°F) and boils at 212°F.
Length and Distance 10 millimeters (mm) = 1 centimeter (cm) 100 centimeters = 1 meter (m) 1,000 meters = 1 kilometer (km)	**Length and Distance** 12 inches (in.) = 1 foot (ft) 3 feet = 1 yard (yd) 5,280 feet = 1 mile (mi)
Volume 1 cubic centimeter (cm^3) = 1 milliliter (mL) 1,000 milliliters = 1 liter (L)	**Volume of Fluids** 8 fluid ounces (fl oz) = 1 cup (c) 2 cups = 1 pint (pt) 2 pints = 1 quart (qt) 4 quarts = 1 gallon (gal)
Mass 1,000 milligrams (mg) = 1 gram (g) 1,000 grams = 1 kilogram (kg)	**Weight** 16 ounces (oz) = 1 pound (lb) 2,000 pounds = 1 ton (T)
Area 1 square kilometer (km^2) =1 km x 1 km 1 hectare = 10,000 square meters (m^2)	**Rate** mph = miles per hour
Rate m/s = meters per second km/h = kilometers per hour	
Force 1 newton (N) = 1 kg x 1m/s^2	

Use a Hand Lens

You use a hand lens to magnify an object, or make the object look larger. With a hand lens, you can see details that would be hard to see without the hand lens.

Magnify a Piece of Cereal

1. Place a piece of your favorite cereal on a flat surface. Look at the cereal carefully. Draw a picture of it.
2. Hold the hand lens so that it is just above the cereal. Look through the lens, and slowly move it away from the cereal. The cereal will look larger.
3. Keep moving the hand lens until the cereal begins to look blurry. Then move the lens a little closer to the cereal until you can see it clearly.
4. Draw a picture of the cereal as you see it through the hand lens. Fill in details that you did not see before.
5. Repeat this activity using objects you are studying in science. It might be a rock, some soil, a seed, or something else.

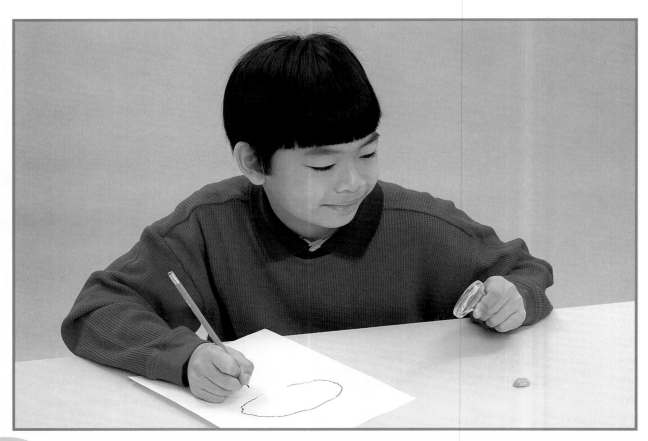

Use a Microscope

Hand lenses make objects look several times larger. A microscope, however, can magnify an object to look hundreds of times larger.

Examine Salt Grains

1. Place the microscope on a flat surface. Always carry a microscope with both hands. Hold the arm with one hand, and put your other hand beneath the base.
2. Look at the drawing to learn the different parts of the microscope.
3. Move the mirror so that it reflects light up toward the stage. Never point the mirror directly at the Sun or a bright light. Bright light can cause permanent eye damage.
4. Place a few grains of salt on the slide. Put the slide under the stage clips on the stage. Be sure that the salt grains are over the hole in the stage.
5. Look through the eyepiece. Turn the focusing knob slowly until the salt grains come into focus.
6. Draw what the grains look like through the microscope.
7. Look at other objects through the microscope. Try a piece of leaf, a strand of human hair, or a pencil mark.
8. Draw what each object looks like through the microscope. Do any of the objects look alike? If so, how? Are any of the objects alive? How do you know?

Eyepiece

Arm

Stage clip

Stage

Focusing knob

Mirror

Base

Measure Time

You use timing devices to measure how long something takes to happen. Some timing devices you use in science are a clock with a second hand and a stopwatch. Which one is more accurate?

Comparing a Clock and a Stopwatch

1. Look at a clock with a second hand. The second hand is the hand that you can see moving. It measures seconds.

2. Get an egg timer with falling sand. When the second hand of the clock points to 12, tell your partner to start the egg timer. Watch the clock while the sand in the egg timer is falling.

3. When the sand stops falling, count how many seconds it took. Record this measurement. Repeat the activity, and compare the two measurements.

4. Look at a stopwatch. Click the button on the top right. This starts the time. Click the button again. This stops the time. Click the button on the top left. This sets the stopwatch back to zero. Notice that the stopwatch tells time in hours, minutes, seconds, and hundredths of a second.

5. Repeat the activity in steps 1–3, but use the stopwatch instead of a clock. Make sure the stopwatch is set to zero. Click the top right button to start timing. Click the

button again when the sand stops falling. Make sure you and your partner time the sand twice.

0 minutes   25 seconds   72 hundredths of a second

More About Time

1. Use the stopwatch to time how long it takes an ice cube to melt under cold running water. How long does an ice cube take to melt under warm running water?

2. Match each of these times with the action you think took that amount of time.

a.   b.   c.

1. A Little League baseball game
2. Saying the Pledge of Allegiance
3. Recess

Measure Length

Find Length with a Ruler

1. Look at this section of a ruler. Each centimeter is divided into 10 millimeters. How long is the paper clip?

2. The length of the paper clip is 3 centimeters plus 2 millimeters. You can write this length as 3.2 centimeters.

3. Place a ruler on your desk. Lay a pencil against the ruler so that one end of the pencil lines up with the left edge of the ruler. Record the length of the pencil.

4. Trade pencils with a classmate. Measure and record the length of each other's pencils. Compare your answers.

Measuring Area

Area is the amount of surface something covers. To find the area of a rectangle, multiply the rectangle's length by its width. For example, the rectangle here is 3 centimeters long and 2 centimeters wide. Its area is 3 cm x 2 cm = 6 square centimeters. You write the area as 6 cm^2.

1. Find the area of your science book. Measure the book's length to the nearest centimeter. Measure its width.

2. Multiply the book's length by its width. Remember to put the answer in cm^2.

1
2
3 ┄┄┄ 3.2 cm
4
5
6
7   10 millimeters = 1 centimeter
8
9

2 cm

◄— 3 cm —►

Measure Mass

Mass is the amount of matter an object has. You use a balance to measure mass. To find the mass of an object, you balance it with objects whose masses you know. Let's find the mass of a box of crayons.

Measure the Mass of a Box of Crayons

1. Place the balance on a flat, level surface.
2. Make sure the empty pans are balanced with each other. The pointer should point to the middle mark. If it does not, move the slider a little to the right or left to balance the pans.
3. Gently place a box of crayons on the left pan.
4. Add masses to the right pan until the pans are balanced.
5. Count the numbers on the masses that are in the right pan. The total is the mass of the box of crayons, in grams. Record this number. After the number, write a *g* for "grams."

More About Mass

What would happen if you replaced the crayons with a pineapple? You may not have enough masses to balance the pineapple. It has a mass of about 1,000 grams. That's the same as 1 kilogram, because *kilo* means "1,000."

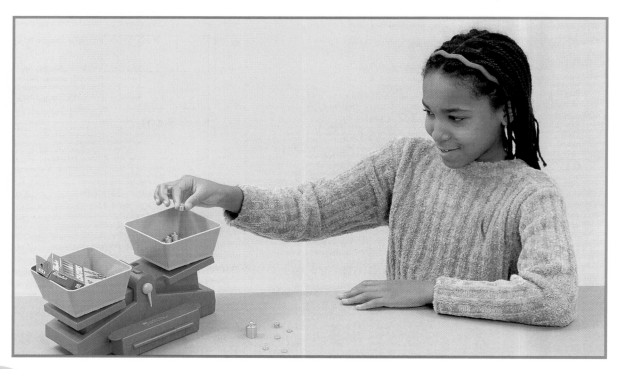

Make Measurements

Measure Volume

Have you ever used a measuring cup? Measuring cups measure the volume of liquids. Volume is the amount of space something takes up. In science you use special measuring cups called beakers and graduated cylinders. These containers are marked in milliliters (mL).

Measure the Volume of a Liquid

1. Look at the beaker and at the graduated cylinder. The beaker has marks for each 25 mL up to 200 mL. The graduated cylinder has marks for each 1 mL up to 100 mL.
2. The surface of the water in the graduated cylinder curves up at the sides. You measure the volume by reading the height of the water at the flat part. What is the volume of water in the graduated cylinder? How much water is in the beaker?
3. Pour 50 mL of water from a pitcher into a graduated cylinder. The water should be at the 50-mL mark on the graduated cylinder. If you go over the mark, pour a little water back into the pitcher.
4. Pour the 50 mL of water into a beaker.
5. Repeat steps 3 and 4 using 30 mL, 45 mL, and 25 mL of water.
6. Measure the volume of water you have in the beaker. Do you have about the same amount of water as your classmates?

Measure Weight/Force

You use a spring scale to measure weight. An object has weight because the force of gravity pulls down on the object. Therefore, weight is a force. Like all forces, weight is measured in newtons (N).

Measure the Weight of an Object

1. Look at your spring scale to see how many newtons it measures. See how the measurements are divided. The spring scale shown here measures up to 10 N. It has a mark for every 1 N.

2. Hold the spring scale by the top loop. Put the object to be measured on the bottom hook. If the object will not stay on the hook, place it in a net bag. Then hang the bag from the hook.

3. Let go of the object slowly. It will pull down on a spring inside the scale. The spring is connected to a pointer. The pointer on the spring scale shown here is a small arrow.

4. Wait for the pointer to stop moving. Read the number of newtons next to the pointer. This is the object's weight. The mug in the picture weighs 3 N.

More About Spring Scales

You probably weigh yourself by standing on a bathroom scale. This is a spring scale. The force of your body stretches a spring inside the scale. The dial on the scale is probably marked in pounds—the English unit of weight. One pound is equal to about 4.5 newtons.

Here are some spring scales you may have seen.

Measure Temperature

Temperature is how hot or cold something is. You use a thermometer to measure temperature. A thermometer is made of a thin tube with colored liquid inside. When the liquid gets warmer, it expands and moves up the tube. When the liquid gets cooler, it contracts and moves down the tube. You may have seen most temperatures measured in degrees Fahrenheit (°F). Scientists measure temperature in degrees Celsius (°C).

Read a Thermometer

1. Look at the thermometer shown here. It has two scales—a Fahrenheit scale and a Celsius scale. Every 20 degrees on each scale has a number.
2. What is the temperature shown on the thermometer? At what temperature does water freeze? Give your answers in °F and in °C.

How Is Temperature Measured?

1. Fill a large beaker about one-half full of cool water. Find the temperature of the water by holding a thermometer in the water. Do not let the bulb at the bottom of the thermometer touch the sides or bottom of the beaker.
2. Keep the thermometer in the water until the liquid in the tube stops moving— about a minute. Read and record the temperature on the Celsius scale.

3. Fill another large beaker one-half full of warm water from a faucet. Be careful not to burn yourself by using hot water.
4. Find and record the temperature of the warm water just as you did in steps 1 and 2.

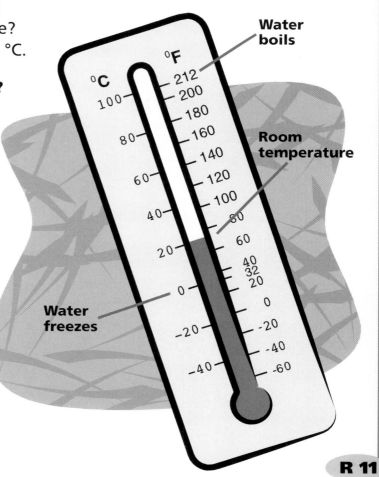

SCIENCE • HANDBOOK

R 11

Use Calculators: Add and Subtract

Sometimes after you make measurements, you have to add or subtract your numbers. A calculator helps you do this.

Add and Subtract Rainfall Amounts

The table shows the amount of rain that fell in a town each week during the summer.

Week	Rain (cm)
1	3
2	5
3	2
4	0
5	1
6	6
7	4
8	0
9	2
10	2
11	6
12	5

1. Make sure the calculator is on. Press the **ON** key.
2. To add the numbers, enter a number and press **+** . Repeat until you enter the last number. Then press **=** . You do not have to enter the zeros. Your total should be 36.

3. What if you found out that you made a mistake in your measurement? Week 1 should be 2 cm less, week 6 should be 3 cm less, week 11 should be 1 cm less, and week 12 should be 2 cm less. Subtract these numbers from your total. You should have 36 displayed on the calculator. Press **−** , and enter the first number you want to subtract. Repeat until you enter the last number. Then press **=** .

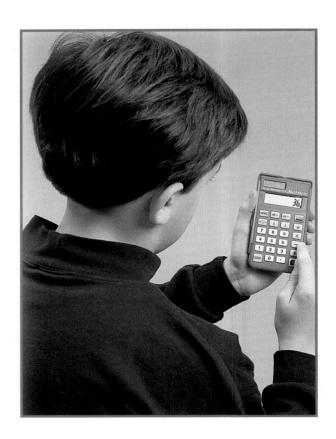

Use Calculators: Multiply and Divide

Sometimes after you make measurements, you have to multiply or divide your measurements to get other information. A calculator helps you multiply and divide, especially if the numbers have decimal points.

Multiply Decimals

What if you are measuring the width of your classroom? You discover that the floor is covered with tiles and the room is exactly 32 tiles wide. You measure a tile, and it is 22.7 centimeters wide. To find the width of the room, you can multiply 32 by 22.7.

1. Make sure the calculator is on. Press the **ON** key.
2. Press **3** and **2**.
3. Press **×**.
4. Press **2**, **2**, **·**, and **7**.
5. Press **=**. Your total should be 726.4. That is how wide the room is in centimeters.

Divide Decimals

Now what if you wanted to find out how many desks placed side by side would be needed to reach across the room? You measure one desk, and it is 60 centimeters wide. To find the number of desks needed, divide 726.4 by 60.

1. Turn the calculator on.
2. Press **7**, **2**, **6**, **·**, and **4**.
3. Press **÷**.
4. Press **6** and **0**.
5. Press **=**. Your total should be about 12.1. This means you can fit 12 desks across the room with a little space left over.

What if the room was 35 tiles wide? How wide would the room be? How many desks would fit across it?

Use Computers

A computer has many uses. The Internet connects your computer to many other computers around the world, so you can collect all kinds of information. You can use a computer to show this information and write reports. Best of all, you can use a computer to explore, discover, and learn.

You can also get information from CD-ROMs. They are computer disks that can hold large amounts of information. You can fit a whole encyclopedia on one CD-ROM.

Use Computers for a Project

Here is how one group of students uses computers as they work on a weather project.

1. The students use instruments to measure temperature, wind speed, wind direction, and other parts of the weather. They input this information, or data, into the computer. The students keep the data in a table. This helps them compare the data from one day to the next.

2. The teacher finds out that another group of students in a town 200 kilometers to the west is also doing a weather project. The two groups use the Internet to talk to each other and share data. When a storm happens in the town to the west, that group tells the other group that it's coming its way.

Use Technology

email: It's going to storm here. The sky is turning dark gray. The winds are sometimes 65 km per hour from the northwest.

3. The students want to find out more. They decide to stay on the Internet and send questions to a local TV weather forecaster. She has a website and answers questions from students every day.

4. Meanwhile some students go to the library to gather more information from a CD-ROM disk. The CD-ROM has an encyclopedia that includes movie clips with sound. The clips give examples of different kinds of storms.

5. The students have kept all their information in a folder called Weather Project. Now they use that information to write a report about the weather. On the computer they can move paragraphs, add words, take out words, put in diagrams, and draw their own weather maps. Then they print the report in color.

6. Use the information on these two pages to plan your own investigation. Use a computer, the Internet, a CD-ROM, or any other technological device.

Make Graphs to Organize Data

When you do an experiment in science, you collect information. To find out what your information means, you can organize it into graphs. There are many kinds of graphs.

Bar Graphs

A bar graph uses bars to show information. For example, what if you are growing a plant? Every week you measure how high the plant has grown. Here is what you find.

Week	Height (cm)
1	1
2	3
3	6
4	10
5	17
6	20
7	22
8	23

The bar graph at right organizes the measurements you collected so that you can easily compare them.

1. Look at the bar for week 2. Put your finger at the top of the bar. Move your finger straight over to the left to find how many centimeters the plant grew by the end of week 2.
2. Between which two weeks did the plant grow most?
3. When did plant growth begin to level off?

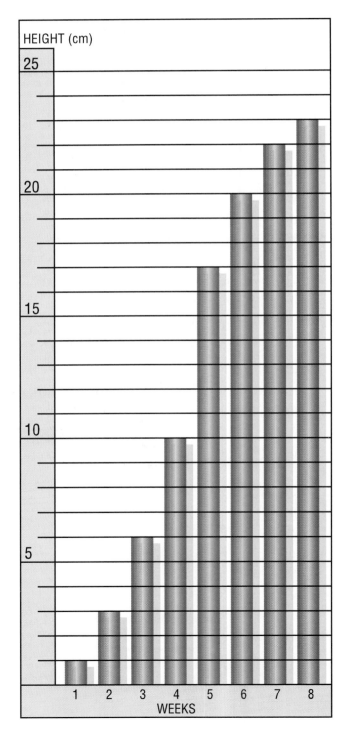

Represent Data

Pictographs

A pictograph uses symbols, or pictures, to show information. What if you collect information about how much water your family uses each day? Here is what you find.

Activity	Water Used Each Day (L)
Drinking	10
Showering	100
Bathing	120
Brushing teeth	40
Washing dishes	80
Washing hands	30
Washing clothes	160
Flushing toilet	50

You can organize this information into the pictograph shown here. In this pictograph each bottle means 20 liters of water. A half bottle means half of 20, or 10 liters of water.

1. Which activity uses the most water?
2. Which activity uses the least water?

Line Graphs

A line graph shows information by connecting dots plotted on the graph. It shows change over time. What if you measure the temperature outdoors every hour starting at 6 A.M.? Here is what you find.

Time	Temperature (°C)
6 A.M.	10
7 A.M.	12
8 A.M.	14
9 A.M.	16
10 A.M.	18
11 A.M.	20

You can organize this information into a line graph. Follow these steps.

1. Make a scale along the bottom and side of the graph. The scales should include all the numbers in the chart. Label the scales.
2. Plot points on the graph.
3. Connect the points with a line.

A Family's Daily Use of Water

= 20 liters of water

Drinking	
Showering	
Bathing	
Brushing teeth	
Washing dishes	
Washing hands	
Washing clothes	
Flushing toilet	

Represent Data

Make Maps, Tables, Charts

Locate Places

A map is a drawing that shows an area from above. Most maps have numbers and letters along the top and side. What if you wanted to find the library on the map below? It is located at D7. Place a finger on the letter D along the side of the map and another finger on the number 7 at the top. Then move your fingers straight across and down the map until they meet. The library is located where D and 7 meet.

1. What building is located at G3?
2. The hospital is located three blocks south and three blocks east of the library. What is its number and letter?
3. Make a map of an area in your community. It might be a park or the area between your home and school. Include numbers and letters along the top and side. Use a compass to find north, and mark north on your map. Exchange maps with classmates.

Idea Maps

The map below left shows how places are connected to each other. Idea maps, on the other hand, show how ideas are connected to each other. Idea maps help you organize information about a topic.

Look at the idea map below. It connects ideas about water. This map shows that Earth's water is either fresh water or salt water. The map also shows four sources of fresh water. You can see that there is no connection between "rivers" and "salt water" on the map. This reminds you that salt water does not flow in rivers.

Make an idea map about a topic you are learning in science. Your map can include words, phrases, or even sentences. Arrange your map in a way that makes sense to you and helps you understand the ideas.

North

	1	2	3	4	5	6	7	8	9	10
A										
B										
C										
D							Library			
E										
F			Store							Hospital
G										

West   East

South

Represent Data

Make Tables and Charts to Organize Data

Tables help to organize data during experiments. Most tables have columns that run up and down, and rows that run across. The columns and rows have headings that tell you what kind of data goes in each part of the table.

A Sample Table

What if you are going to do an experiment to find out how long different kinds of seeds take to sprout? Before you begin the experiment, you should set up your table. Follow these steps.

1. In this experiment you will plant 20 radish seeds, 20 bean seeds, and 20 corn seeds. Your table must show how many of each kind of seed sprouted on days 1, 2, 3, 4, and 5.

2. Make your table with columns, rows, and headings. You might use a computer. Some computer programs let you build a table with just the click of a mouse. You can delete or add columns and rows if you need to.

3. Give your table a title. Your table could look like the one here.

TYPES OF SEEDS	NUMBER OF SEEDS THAT SPROUT				
	DAY 1	DAY 2	DAY 3	DAY 4	DAY 5
Radish seeds					
Bean seeds					
Corn seeds					

Make a Table

Plant 20 bean seeds in each of two trays. Keep each tray at a different temperature, as shown above, and observe the trays for seven days. Make a table that you can use for this experiment. You can use the table to record, examine, and evaluate the information of this experiment.

Make a Chart

A chart is simply a table with pictures, as well as words to label the rows or columns. Make a chart that shows the information of the above experiment.

The Skeletal System

The body has a supporting frame, called a skeleton, which is made up of bones. The skeleton has several jobs.

- It gives the body its shape.
- It protects organs in the body.
- It works with muscles to move the body.

Each of the 206 bones of the skeleton is the size and shape best fitted to do its job. For example, long and strong leg bones support the body's weight.

The Skeleton

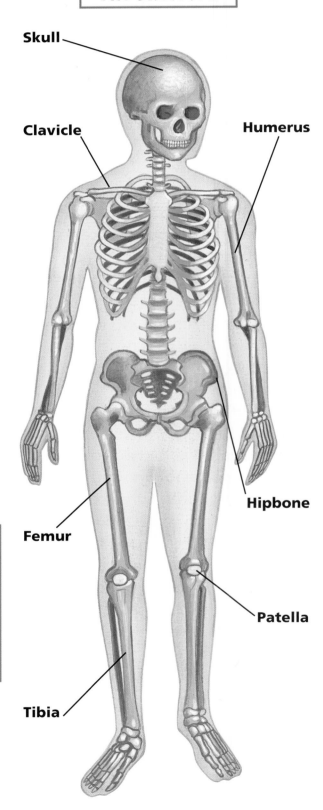

Skull

Clavicle

Humerus

Femur

Hipbone

Patella

Tibia

CARE!

- Exercise to keep your skeletal system in good shape.
- Don't overextend your joints.

Bones

1 A bone is covered with a tough but thin membrane that has many small blood vessels. The blood vessels bring nutrients and oxygen to the living parts of the bone and remove wastes.

2 Inside some bones is a soft tissue known as marrow. Yellow marrow is made mostly of fat cells and is one of the body's energy reserves. It is usually found in the long, hollow spaces of long bones.

3 Part of the bone is compact, or solid. It is made up of living bone cells and non-living materials. The nonliving part is made up of layers of hardened minerals such as calcium and phosphorus. In between the mineral layers are living bone cells.

4 Red marrow fills the spaces in spongy bone. Red marrow makes new red blood cells, germ-fighting white blood cells, and cell fragments that stop a cut from bleeding.

5 Part of the bone is made of bone tissue that looks like a dry sponge. It is made of strong, hard tubes. It is also found in the middle of short, flat bones.

CARE!

- **Eat foods rich in vitamins and minerals. Your bones need the minerals calcium and phosphorus to grow strong.**
- **Be careful! Avoid sprains and fractures.**
- **Get help in case of injury.**

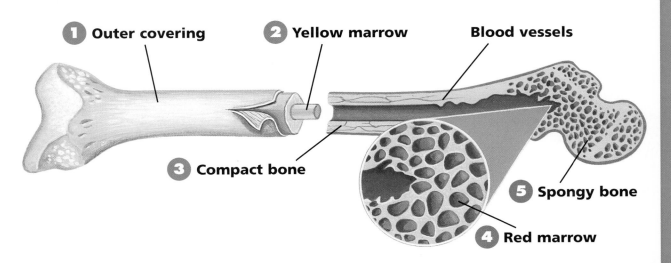

1 Outer covering   **2** Yellow marrow   Blood vessels
3 Compact bone   **5** Spongy bone   **4** Red marrow

Joints

The skeleton has different types of joints. A joint is a place where two or more bones meet. Joints can be classified into three major groups—immovable joints, partly movable joints, and movable joints.

Types of Joints

IMMOVABLE JOINTS

Head

Immovable joints are places where bones fit together too tightly to move. Nearly all the 29 bones in the skull meet at immovable joints. Only the lower jaw can move.

PARTLY MOVABLE JOINTS

Partly movable joints are places where bones can move only a little. Ribs are connected to the breastbone with these joints.

Ribs

Breastbone

MOVABLE JOINTS

Movable joints are places where bones can move easily.

Gliding joint

Hand and wrist

Small bones in the wrists and ankles meet at gliding joints. The bones can slide against one another. These joints allow some movement in all directions.

The hips are examples of ball-and-socket joints. The ball of one bone fits into the socket, or cup, of another bone. These joints allow bones to move back and forth, in a circle, and side to side.

Ball-and-socket joint

Hip

Hinge joint

Knee

The knees are hinge joints. A hinge joint is similar to a door hinge. It allows bones to move back and forth in one direction.

The joint between the skull and neck is a pivot joint. It allows the head to move up and down, and side to side.

Pivot joint

Neck

The Muscular System

1. A message from your brain causes this muscle, called the biceps, to contract. When a muscle contracts, it becomes shorter and thicker. As the biceps contracts, it pulls on the arm bone it is attached to.

2. Most muscles work in pairs to move bones. This muscle, called the triceps, relaxes when the biceps contracts. When a muscle relaxes, it becomes longer and thinner.

3. To straighten your arm, a message from your brain causes the triceps to contract. When the triceps contracts, it pulls on the bone it is attached to.

4. As the triceps contracts, the biceps relaxes. Your arm straightens.

Three types of muscles make up the body—skeletal muscle, cardiac muscle, and smooth muscle.

The muscles that are attached to and move bones are called skeletal muscles. These muscles are attached to bones by a tough cord called a tendon. Skeletal muscles pull bones to move them. Muscles do not push bones.

Cardiac muscles are found in only one place in the body—the heart. The walls of the heart are made of strong cardiac muscles. When cardiac muscles contract, they squeeze blood out of the heart. When cardiac muscles relax, the heart fills with more blood.

Smooth muscles make up internal organs and blood vessels. Smooth muscles in the lungs help a person breathe. Those in the blood vessels help control blood flow around the body.

CARE!

- Exercise to strengthen your muscles.
- Eat the right foods.
- Get plenty of rest.

The Circulatory System

The circulatory system consists of the heart, blood vessels, and blood. Circulation is the flow of blood through the body. Blood is a liquid that contains red blood cells, white blood cells, and platelets. Red blood cells carry oxygen and nutrients to cells. White blood cells work to fight germs that enter the body. Platelets are cell fragments that make the blood clot.

The heart is a muscular organ about the size of a fist. It beats about 70 to 90 times a minute, pumping blood through the blood vessels. Arteries carry blood away from the heart. Some arteries carry blood to the lungs, where the cells pick up oxygen. Other arteries carry oxygen-rich blood from the lungs to all other parts of the body. Veins carry blood from other parts of the body back to the heart. Blood in most veins carries the wastes released by cells and has little oxygen. Blood flows from arteries to veins through narrow vessels called capillaries.

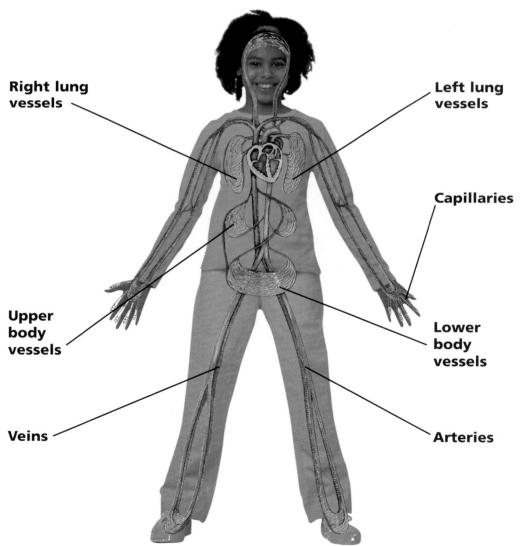

Right lung vessels

Left lung vessels

Capillaries

Upper body vessels

Lower body vessels

Veins

Arteries

The Heart

The heart has two sides, right and left, separated by a thick muscular wall. Each side has two chambers for blood. The upper chamber is the atrium. The lower chamber is the ventricle. Blood enters the heart through the vena cava. It leaves the heart through the aorta.

The pulmonary artery carries blood from the body into the lungs. Here carbon dioxide leaves the blood to be exhaled by the lungs. Fresh oxygen enters the blood to be carried to every cell in the body. Blood returns from the lungs to the heart through the pulmonary veins.

CARE!

- Don't smoke. The nicotine in tobacco makes the heart beat faster and work harder to pump blood.

- Never take illegal drugs, such as cocaine or heroin. They can damage the heart and cause heart failure.

To the Lungs

1 The right atrium fills.

Right atrium

2 Right atrium squeezes blood into right ventricle.

3 Right ventricle squeezes blood into pulmonary artery.

One-way valve

Right ventricle

How the Heart Works

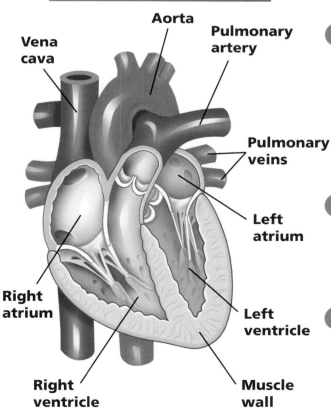

Vena cava

Aorta

Pulmonary artery

Pulmonary veins

Left atrium

Right atrium

Right ventricle

Left ventricle

Muscle wall

From the Lungs

1 The left atrium fills.

2 Left atrium squeezes blood into left ventricle.

3 Left ventricle squeezes blood into aorta.

Left atrium

One-way valve

Left ventricle

The Respiratory System

The process of getting and using oxygen in the body is called respiration. When a person inhales, air is pulled into the nose or mouth. The air travels down into the trachea. In the chest the trachea divides into two bronchial tubes. One bronchial tube enters each lung. Each bronchial tube branches into smaller tubes called bronchioles.

At the end of each bronchiole are tiny air sacs called alveoli. The alveoli exchange carbon dioxide for oxygen.

Oxygen comes from the air we breathe. Two muscles control breathing, the lungs and a dome-shaped sheet of muscle called the diaphragm.

To inhale, the diaphragm contracts and pulls down. To exhale, the diaphragm relaxes and returns to its dome shape.

CARE!

- **Don't smoke. Smoking damages your respiratory system.**

- **Exercise to strengthen your breathing muscles.**

- **If you ever have trouble breathing, tell an adult at once.**

Air Flow

Carbon dioxide | Oxygen

Carbon dioxide diffuses into the alveoli. From there it is exhaled.

Capillary net

Oxygen → Carbon dioxide ←

Diaphragm

The air you breathe is about 21 percent oxygen.

The blood in the capillaries of your lungs has very little oxygen.

The blood has a higher concentration of carbon dioxide than air.

Throat

Trachea

Alveoli

Fresh oxygen diffuses from the alveoli to the blood.

Lungs

Activity Pyramid

Physical fitness is the condition in which the body is healthy and works the best it can. It involves working the skeletal muscles, bones, joints, heart, and respiratory system.

3–5 times a week
Aerobic activities such as swimming, biking, climbing; sports activities such as basketball, handball

Occasionally
Inactive pastimes such as watching TV, playing board games, talking on the phone

2–3 times a week
Leisure activities such as gardening, golf, softball

The activity pyramid shows you the kinds of exercises and other activities you should be doing to make your body more physically fit.

Daily Substitute activity for inactivity— take the stairs, walk instead of riding, bike instead of taking the bus

Food Guide Pyramid

To make sure the body stays fit and healthy, a person needs to eat a balanced diet. The Food Guide Pyramid shows how many servings of each group a person should eat every day.

CARE!

- **Stay active every day.**
- **Eat a balanced diet.**
- **Drink plenty of water— 6 to 8 large glasses a day.**

Fats, oils, and sweets
Use sparingly

Milk, yogurt, and cheese group
2–3 servings

Meat, dry beans, eggs, and nuts group
2–3 servings

Vegetable group
3–5 servings

Fruit group
2–4 servings

Bread, cereal, rice, and pasta group
6–11 servings

The Digestive System

Digestion is the process of breaking down food into simple substances the body can use. Digestion begins when a person chews food. Chewing breaks the food down into smaller pieces and moistens it with saliva. Saliva is produced by the salivary glands.

Digested food is absorbed in the small intestine. The walls of the small intestine are lined with villi. Villi are tiny fingerlike projections that absorb digested food. From the villi the blood transports nutrients to every part of the body.

CARE!

- Chew your food well.
- Drink plenty of water to help move food through your digestive system.

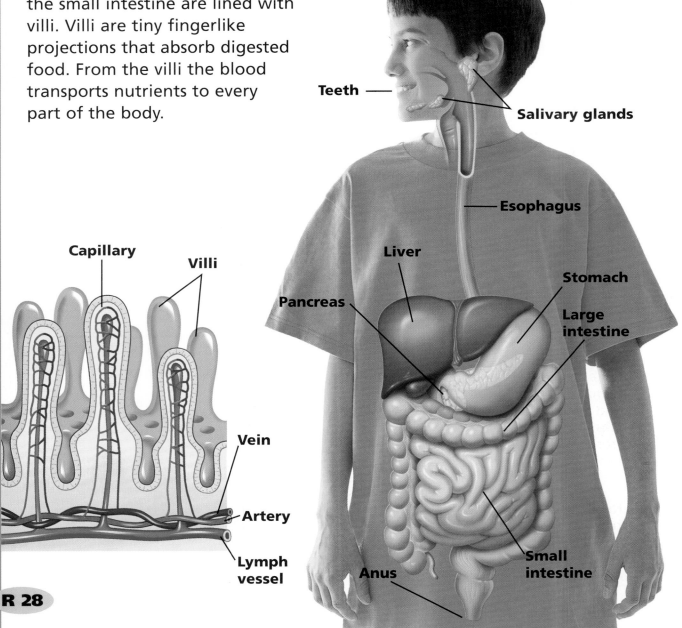

Capillary

Villi

Teeth

Salivary glands

Esophagus

Liver

Stomach

Pancreas

Large intestine

Vein

Artery

Lymph vessel

Anus

Small intestine

The Excretory System

Excretion is the process of removing waste products from the body. The liver filters wastes from the blood and converts them into urea. Urea is then carried to the kidneys for excretion.

The skin takes part in excretion when a person sweats. Glands in the inner layer of the skin produce sweat. Sweat is mostly water. Sweat tastes salty because it contains mineral salts the body doesn't need. There is also a tiny amount of urea in sweat.

Sweat is excreted onto the outer layer of the skin. Evaporation into the air takes place in part because of body heat. When sweat evaporates, a person feels cooler.

How You Sweat

Glands under your skin push sweat up to the surface, where it collects.

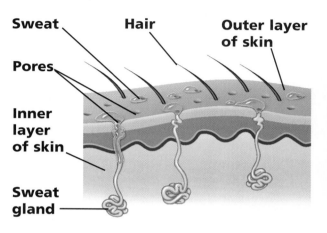

Sweat • Hair • Outer layer of skin • Pores • Inner layer of skin • Sweat gland

CARE!

● Wash regularly to avoid body odor, clogged pores, and skin irritation.

How Your Kidneys Work

1 Blood enters the kidney through an artery and flows into capillaries.

2 Sugars, salts, water, urea, and other wastes move from the capillaries to tiny nephrons.

3 Nutrients return to the blood and flow back out through veins.

4 Urea and other wastes become urine, which flows down the ureters.

5 Urine is stored in the bladder and excreted through the urethra.

Artery • Vein • Capillaries

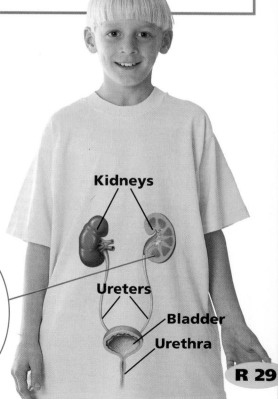

Kidneys • Ureters • Bladder • Urethra

The Nervous System

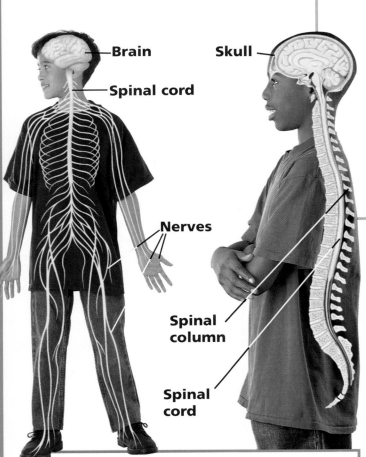

Brain

Spinal cord

Nerves

Spinal column

Spinal cord

Skull

Cerebrum

Movement
Reason
Touch
Speech   Hearing
Taste
Smell   Vision
Balance

Heartbeat   Cerebellum
Breathing

Medulla

CARE!

- To protect the brain and spinal cord, wear protective headgear when you play sports or exercise.

- Stay away from alcohol, which is a depressant and slows down the nervous system.

- Stay away from drugs, such as stimulants, which can speed up the nervous system.

The nervous system has two parts. The brain and the spinal cord are the central nervous system. All other nerves are the outer nervous system.

The largest part of the brain is the cerebrum. A deep groove separates the right half, or hemisphere, of the cerebrum from the left half. Both sides of the cerebrum contain control centers for the senses.

The cerebellum lies below the cerebrum. It coordinates the skeletal muscles. It also helps in keeping balance.

The brain stem connects to the spinal cord. The lowest part of the brain stem is the medulla. It controls heartbeat, breathing, blood pressure, and the muscles in the digestive system.

The Endocrine System

Hormones are chemicals that control body functions. A gland that produces hormones is called an endocrine gland. Sweat from sweat glands flows out of tubes called ducts. Endocrine glands have no ducts.

The endocrine glands are scattered around the body. Each gland makes one or more hormones. Every hormone seeks out a target organ. This is the place in the body where the hormone acts.

Some Glands in the Endocrine System

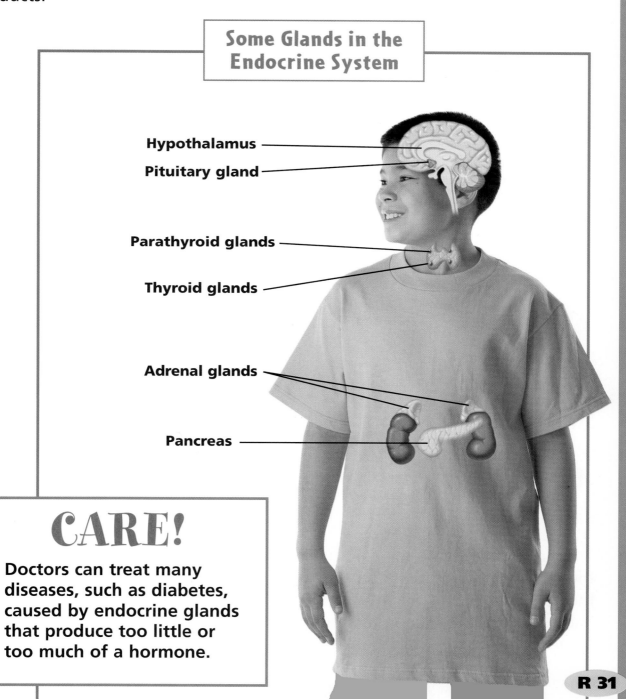

Hypothalamus

Pituitary gland

Parathyroid glands

Thyroid glands

Adrenal glands

Pancreas

CARE!

• Doctors can treat many diseases, such as diabetes, caused by endocrine glands that produce too little or too much of a hormone.

The Senses

Seeing

Retina
Cornea
Optic nerve
Iris
Lens

Light reflected from an object enters the eye and falls on the retina. Receptor cells change the light into electrical signals, or impulses. These impulses travel along the optic nerve to the vision center of the brain.

1 Light reflects off the tree and into your eyes.

2 The light passes through your cornea and the pupil in your iris.

3 Your eye bends the light so it hits your retina.

4 Receptor cells on your retina change the light into electrical signals.

5 The impulses travel along neurons in your optic nerve to the seeing center of your brain.

Hearing

1 Your outer ear collects sound waves.

2 They are funneled down your ear canal.

3 The eardrum vibrates.

4 Three tiny ear bones vibrate.

5 The cochlea vibrates.

6 Receptor cells inside your cochlea change.

7 The impulses travel along your auditory nerve to the brain's hearing center.

Hammer
Auditory nerve
Hearing center
Eardrum
Anvil
Stirrup
Cochlea

Sound waves enter the ear and cause the eardrum to vibrate. Receptor cells in the ear change the sound waves into impulses that travel along the auditory nerve to the hearing center of the brain.

CARE!

- **Avoid loud music.**
- **Don't sit too close to the TV screen.**

The Senses

Smelling

The sense of smell is really the ability to detect chemicals in the air. When a person breathes, chemicals dissolve in mucus in the upper part of the nose. When the chemicals come in contact with receptor cells, the cells send impulses along the olfactory nerve to the smelling center of the brain.

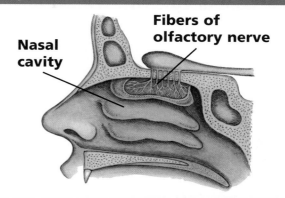

Nasal cavity

Fibers of olfactory nerve

Tasting

When a person eats, chemicals in food dissolve in saliva. Inside each taste bud are receptors that can sense the four main tastes—sweet, sour, salty, and bitter. The receptors send impulses along a nerve to the taste center of the brain. The brain identifies the taste of the food.

Bitter
Sour
Salty
Sweet

Touching

Receptor cells in the skin help a person tell hot from cold, wet from dry, and the light touch of a feather from the pressure of stepping on a stone. Each receptor cell sends impulses along sensory nerves to the spinal cord. The spinal cord then sends the impulses to the touch center of the brain.

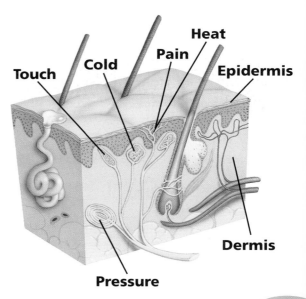

Touch
Cold
Pain
Heat
Epidermis
Dermis
Pressure

CARE!

- To prevent the spread of germs, always cover your mouth and nose when you cough or sneeze.

The Immune System

The immune system helps the body fight disease. When a person has a cut, germ-fighting white blood cells rush to the wound. There are white blood cells in the blood vessels and in the lymph vessels. Lymph vessels are similar to blood vessels. Instead of blood, they carry lymph. Lymph is a straw-colored fluid surrounding body cells.

Lymph nodes filter out harmful materials in the body. They also produce white blood cells to fight infections. Swollen lymph nodes in the neck are a clue that the body is fighting germs.

Lymph node   **Lymph vessels**

Lymph vessels

Lymph nodes

Lymph vessels run through your body to collect fluid and return it to the bloodstream.

CARE!

- **Be sure to get immunized against common diseases.**
- **Keep cuts clean to prevent infection.**

Glossary

This Glossary will help you to pronounce and understand the meanings of the Science Words introduced in this book. The page number at the end of the definition tells where the word appears.

A

adaptation (ad′əp tā′shən) A special characteristic that helps an organism survive. (p. B50)

air (âr) A mixture of gases and dust. (p. D6)

air pressure (âr presh′ər) The force of air pushing down on Earth. (p. D9)

algae (al′jē) *pl. n., sing.* (-gə) Tiny one-celled organisms. (pp. B9, B27)

amber (am′bər) Hardened tree sap, often a source of insect fossils. (p. C22)

amphibian (am fib′ē ən) An animal that spends part of its life in water and part of its life on land. (p. A72)

anemometer (an′ə mom′i tər) A device that measures wind speed. (p. D25)

aqueduct (ak′wə dukt′) A pipe or channel for carrying water over long distances. (p. C32)

atmosphere (at′məs fîr′) Gases that surround Earth. (p. D6)

atom (at′əm) The smallest particle of matter. (p. F28)

axis (ak′sis) A real or imaginary line through the center of a spinning object. (p. D37)

PRONUNCIATION KEY

The following symbols are used throughout the McGraw-Hill Science 2002 Glossaries.

a	at	e	end	o	hot	u	up	hw	white	ə about
ā	ape	ē	me	ō	old	ū	use	ng	song	taken
ä	far	i	it	ôr	fork	ü	rule	th	thin	pencil
âr	care	ī	ice	oi	oil	u̇	pull	<u>th</u>	this	lemon
ô	law	îr	pierce	ou	out	ûr	turn	zh	measure	circus

′ = primary accent; shows which syllable takes the main stress, such as **kil** in **kilogram** (kil′ə gram′).

′ = secondary accent; shows which syllables take lighter stresses, such as **gram** in **kilogram**.

bacteria, (bak tîr′ē ə) One-celled living things. (p. B18)

barometer (bə rom′i tər) A device for measuring air pressure. (p. D24)

bird (bûrd) An animal that has a beak, feathers, two wings, and two legs. (p. A73)

bulb (bulb) The underground stem of such plants as onions and irises. (p. A30)

C

camouflage (kam′ə fläzh) An adaptation that allows animals to blend into their surroundings. (p. B52)

carbon dioxide and oxygen cycles (kär′bən dī ok′sīd and ok′sə jən sī′kəlz) The process of passing oxygen and carbon dioxide from one population to another in both water and land habitats. (p. B27)

carnivore (kär′nə vôr′) An animal that eats only other animals. (p. B20)

cast (kast) A fossil formed or shaped inside a mold. (p. C23)

cell (sel) **1.** The basic building block of life. (p. A10) **2.** A source of electricity. (p. F72)

cell membrane (sel mem′brān′) The thin outer covering of a cell. (p. A10)

cell wall (sel wôl) A stiff layer outside the cell membrane of plant cells. (p. A11)

chemical change (kəm′i kəl chānj) A change that forms a different kind of matter. (p. F30)

chloroplast (klôr′ə plast′) One of the small green bodies inside a plant cell that makes foods for the plant. (p. A11)

circuit (sûr′kit) The path electricity flows through. (p. F72)

classify (klas′ə fī) To place materials that share properties together in groups. (p. S7)

communicate (kə mü′ni kāt′) To share information. (p. S7)

community (kə mü′ni tē) All the living things in an ecosystem. (p. B6)

competition (kom′pi tish′ən) The struggle among organisms for water, food, or other needs. (p. B42)

compound (kom′pound) Two or more elements put together. (p. F30)

compound machine (kom′pound mə shēn′) Two or more simple machines put together. (p. E57)

condense (kən dens′) *v.* To change from a gas to a liquid. (pp. C31, F17) —**condensation** (kon′den sā′shən) *n.* (p. D17)

conductor (kən duk′tər) A material that heat travels through easily. (p. F46)

conifer (kon′ə fər) A tree that produces seeds inside of cones. (p. A28)

conserve (kən sûrv′) To save, protect, or use something wisely without wasting it. (p. C34)

consumer (kən sü′mər) An organism that eats producers or other consumers. (pp. A40, B17)

crater (krā′tər) A hollow area in the ground. (p. D49)

cutting (kut′ing) A plant part from which a new plant can grow. (p. A30)

cytoplasm (sī′tə pla′zəm) A clear, jellylike material that fills both plant and animal cells. (p. A10)

D

decibel (dB) (des′ə bel′) A unit that measures loudness. (p. F69)

decomposer (dē′kəm pō′zər) An organism that breaks down dead plant and animal material. *Decomposers* recycle chemicals so they can be used again. (p. B18)

define based on observations (di fīn′ bāst ôn ob′zər vā′shənz) To put together a description that relies on examination and experience. (p. S7)

degree (di grē′) The unit of measurement for temperature. (p. F43)

PRONUNCIATION KEY

a at; ā ape; ä far; âr care; ô law; e end; ē me; i it; ī ice; îr pierce; o hot; ō old; ôr fork; oi oil; ou out; u up; ū use;
ü rule; u̇ pull; ûr turn; hw white; ng song; th thin; th this; zh measure; ə about, taken, pencil, lemon, circus

desert (dez′ərt) A hot dry place with very little rain. (p. B55)

development (di vel′əp mənt) The way a living thing changes during its life. (p. A6)

distance (dis′təns) The length between two places. (p. E7)

E

earthquake (ûrth′kwāk) A sudden movement in the rocks that make up Earth's crust. (p. C72)

ecosystem (ek′ō sis′təm) All the living and nonliving things in an environment and all their interactions. (p. B6)

electric current (i lek′trik kûr′ənt) Electricity that flows through a circuit. (p. F72)

element (el′ə mənt) A building block of matter. (p. F28)

embryo (em′brē ō) A young organism that is just beginning to grow. (p. A26)

endangered (en dān′jərd) Close to becoming extinct; having very few of its kind left. (p. B64)

energy (en′ər jē) The ability to do work. (pp. A18, E39)

energy pyramid (en′ər jē pir′ə mid′) A diagram that shows how energy is used in an ecosystem. (p. B22)

environment (en vī′rən mənt) The things that make up an area, such as land, water, and air. (p. A8)

erosion (i rō′zhən) The carrying away of weathered materials. (p. C62)

evaporate (i vap′ə rāt′) *v.* To change from a liquid to a gas. (pp. C31, F17) —**evaporation** (i vap′ə rā′shən′) *n.* (p. D17)

experiment (ek sper′ə ment′) To perform a test to support or disprove a hypothesis. (p. S7)

extinct (ek stingkt) Died out, leaving no more of that type of organism alive. (p. B66)

F

fertilizer (fûr′tə līz) A substance added to the soil that is used to make plants grow. (p. C42)

first quarter (fûrst kwôr′tər) A phase of the Moon in which the right half is visible and growing larger. (p. D47)

fish (fish) An animal that lives its whole life in water. (p. A71)

glacier (glā′shər) A large mass of ice in motion. (p. C62)

gram (gram) A metric unit used to measure mass; 1,000 *grams* equals 1 kilogram. (p. F9)

gravity (grav′i tē) A pulling force between two objects, such as Earth and you. (p. E16)

groundwater (ground wô′tər) Water stored in the cracks of underground rocks and soil. (p. C33)

H

habitat (hab′i tat) The home of a living thing. (p. B7)

heat (hēt) A form of energy that makes things warmer. (p. F42)

herbivore (hûr′bə vôr′) An animal that eats only plants. (p. B20)

heredity (hə red′i tē) The passing of traits from parents to offspring. (p. A27)

hibernate (hī′bər nāt′) To rest or sleep through the cold winter. (p. A46)

host (hōst). An organism that a parasite lives with. (p. B31)

humus (hü′məs) Leftover decomposed plant and animal matter. (p. C14)

hurricane (hûr′i kān′) A violent storm with strong winds and heavy rains. (p. C70)

igneous rock (ig′nē əs rok) A "fire-made" rock formed from melted rock material. (p. C8)

imprint (im′print′) A shallow mark or print in a rock. (p. C23)

inclined plane (in klīnd′ plān) A flat surface that is raised at one end. (p. E54)

infer (in fûr′) To form an idea from facts or observations. (p. S7)

inherited trait (in her′i təd trāt) A characteristic that comes from your parents. (p. A56)

inner planet (in′ər plan′it) Any of the four planets in the solar system that are closest to the Sun: Mercury, Venus, Earth, and Mars. (p. D56)

insulator (in′sə lā′tər) A material that heat doesn't travel through easily. (p. F46)

interpret data (in tûr'prit dā'tə) To use the information that has been gathered to answer questions or solve a problem. (p. S7)

K

key (kē) A table that shows what different symbols on a map stand for. (p. E10)

kilogram (kil'ə gram') A metric unit used to measure mass; 1 *kilogram* equals 1,000 grams. (p. F9)

L

landform (land'fôrm') A feature on Earth's surface. (p. C54)

last quarter (last kwôr'tər) or **third quarter** (thûrd kwôr'tər) The phase of the waning Moon in which the left half is visible but growing smaller. (p. D47)

leaf (lēf) A plant part that grows from the stem and helps the plant get air and make food. (p. A18)

learned trait (lûrnd trāt) Something that you are taught or learn from experience. (p. A56)

lens (lenz) A curved piece of glass. (p. D58)

lever (lev'ər) A straight bar that moves on a fixed point. (p. E44)

life cycle (līf sī'kəl) All the stages in an organism's life. (p. A26)

liquid (lik'wid) Matter that has a definite volume but not a definite shape. (p. F14)

liter (lē'tər) A metric unit used to measure volume. (p. F9)

load (lōd) The object that a lever lifts or moves. (p. E44)

loam (lōm) A kind of soil that contains clay, sand, silt, and humus. Plants grow well in loam. (p. C15)

luster (lus'tər) How an object reflects light. (p. F6)

PRONUNCIATION KEY

a at; ā ape; ä far; âr care; ô law; e end; ē me; i it; ī ice; îr pierce; o hot; ō old; ôr fork; oi oil; ou out; u up; ū use; ü rule; ù pull; ûr turn; hw white; ng song; th thin; th this; zh measure; ə about, taken, pencil, lemon, circus

machine (mə shēn') A tool that makes work easier to do. (p. E44)

magnetism (mag'ni tiz'əm) The property of an object that makes it attract iron. (p. F26)

make a model (māk ə mod'əl) To make something to represent an object or event. (p. S7)

mammal (mam'əl) An animal with fur that feeds its young with milk. (p. A74)

map (map) A flat drawing that shows the positions of things. (p. E10)

mass (mas) The amount of matter in an object. (p. F7)

matter (mat'ər) Anything that takes up space and has mass. (pp. D16, F6)

measure (mezh'ər) To find the size, volume, area, mass, weight, or temperature of an object, or how long an event occurs. (p. S7)

melt (melt) To change from a solid to a liquid. (p. F17)

metal (met'əl) A shiny material found in the ground. (p. F26)

metamorphic rock (met'ə môr'fik rok) A rock that has changed form through squeezing and heating. (p. C9)

metamorphosis (met'ə môr'fə sis) A change in the body form of an organism. (p. A52)

microscope (mī'krə skōp') A device that uses glass lenses to allow people to see very small things. (p. A10)

migrate (mī'grāt) To move to another place. (p. A46)

mimicry (mim'i krē) The imitation by one animal of the traits of another. (p. B53)

mineral (min'ə rəl) A naturally occurring substance, neither plant nor animal. (pp. A16, C6)

mixture (miks'chər) Different types of matter mixed together. The properties of each kind of matter in the mixture does not change. (p. F18)

mold (mold) An empty space in a rock that once contained an object such as a dead organism. (p. C23)

motion (mō'shən) A change in position. (p. E8)

mountain (moun′tən) The highest of Earth's landforms. *Mountains* often have steep sides and pointed tops. (p. C55)

N

natural resource (nach′ər əl rē′sôrs′) A material on Earth that is necessary or useful to people. (p. C38)

nectar (nek′tər) The sugary liquid in flowers that lures insects that aid in pollination. (p. A28)

new Moon (nü mün) A phase of the Moon in which none of its sunlit half is visible from Earth. (p. D47)

newton (nü′tən) The unit used to measure pushes and pulls. (pp. E17, F10)

niche (nich) The job or role an organism has in an ecosystem. (p. B44)

nonrenewable resource (non′ri nü′ə bəl rē′sôrs′) A resource that cannot be reused or replaced easily. (p. C41)

nucleus (nü′klē əs) The control center of a cell. (p. A11)

O

observe (əb sûrv′) To use one or more of the senses to identify or learn about an object or event. (p. S7)

omnivore (om′nə vôr′) An animal that eats both plants and animals. (p. B21)

opaque (ō pāk′) A material that doesn't allow light to pass through. (p. F54)

orbit (ôr′bit) The path an object follows as it revolves around another object. (p. D38)

organ (ôr′gən) A group of tissues that work together. (p. A62)

PRONUNCIATION KEY

a at; ā ape; ä far; âr care; ô law; e end; ē me; i it; ī ice; îr pierce; o hot; ō old; ôr fork; oi oil; ou out; u up; ū use; ü rule; u̇ pull; ûr turn; hw white; ng song; th thin; <u>th</u> this; zh measure; ə about, taken, pencil, lemon, circus

organism (ôr'gə niz'əm) Any living thing. (p. A6)

outer planet (out'ər plan'it) Any of the five planets in the solar system that are farthest from the Sun: Jupiter, Saturn, Uranus, Neptune, and Pluto. (p. D56)

oxygen (ok'sə jən) A gas that is in air and water. (p. A19)

P

parasite (par'ə sīt'). An organism that lives in or on a host. (p. B31)

perish (per'ish) To fail to survive. (p. B63)

phase (fāz) An apparent change in the Moon's shape. (p. D46)

physical change (fiz'i kəl chānj) A change in the way matter looks that leaves the matter itself unchanged. (p. F16)

pitch (pich) How high or low a sound is. (p. F66)

plain (plān) Wide flat lands. (p. C55)

planet (plan'it) Any of the nine large bodies that orbit the Sun. In order from the Sun outward, they are Mercury, Venus, Earth, Mars, Jupiter, Saturn, Uranus, Neptune, and Pluto. (p. D54)

pollen (pol'ən) A powdery material needed by the eggs of flowers to make seeds. (p. A28)

pollution (pə lü'shən) The adding of harmful substances to the water, air, or land. (p. C42)

population (pop'yə lā'shən) All the members of a single type of organism in an ecosystem. (p. B6)

position (pə zish'ən) The location of an object. (p. E6)

precipitation (pri sip'i tā'shən) Water in the atmosphere that falls to Earth as rain, snow, hail, or sleet. (p. D19)

predator (pred'ə tər) An animal that hunts for food. (p. B28)

predict (pri dikt') To state possible results of an event or experiment. (p. S7)

prey (prā) The animals that predators eat. (p. B28)

prism (pri′zəm) A thick piece of glass that refracts light. (p. F57)

producer (prə dü′sər) An organism such as a plant that makes its own food. (p. B16)

property (prop′ər tē) Any characteristic of matter that you can observe. (p. F6)

pulley (pu̇l′ē) A simple machine that uses a wheel and a rope. (p. E48)

R

rain gauge (rān gāj) A device that measures how much precipitation has fallen. (p. D24)

ramp (ramp) Another name for an inclined plane. (p. E54)

recycle (rē sī′kəl) To treat something so it can be used again. (p. C44)

reduce (ri düs′) To use less of something. (p. C44)

reflect (ri flekt′) The bouncing of light off a surface. (p. F55)

refract (ri frakt′) The bending of light as it passes through matter. (p. F56)

relocate (rē lō′kāt) To find a new home. (p. B63)

renewable resource (ri nü′ə bəl rē′sôrs′) A resource that can be replaced or used over and over again. (p. C40)

reproduction (rē′prə duk′shən) The way organisms make more of their own kind. (p. A7)

reptile (rep′təl′) An animal that lives on land and has waterproof skin. (p. A72)

reservoir (rez′ər vwär′) A storage area for fresh water supplies. (p. C32)

respond (ri spond′) To react to changes in the environment. (p. A8)

reuse (rē ūz′) v. To use something again. (p. C44)

revolve (ri volv′) To move around another object. (p. D38)

PRONUNCIATION KEY

a at; ā ape; ä far; âr care; ô law; e end; ē me; i it; ī ice; îr pierce; o hot; ō old; ôr fork; oi oil; ou out; u up; ū use;
ü rule; u̇ pull; ûr turn; hw white; ng song; th thin; th this; zh measure; ə about, taken, pencil, lemon, circus

river (riv′ər) A large stream of water that flows across the land. (p. C55)

root (rüt) A plant part that takes in water and grows under the ground. (p. A17)

rotate (rō′tāt) To turn around. (p. D36)

S

sand dune (sand dün) A mound of windblown sand. (p. C55)

sapling (sap′ling) A very young tree. (p. A6)

satellite (sat′ə līt′) Any object that orbits another larger body in space. (p. D46)

scavenger (skav′ən jər) An animal that gets its food by eating dead organisms. (p. B29)

screw (skrü) An inclined plane wrapped into a spiral. (p. E56)

sedimentary rock (sed′ə men′tə rē rok) A kind of rock formed when sand, mud, pebbles at the bottom of rivers, lakes, and oceans pile up. (p. C8)

seedling (sēd′ling) A young plant. (p. A27)

shelter (shel′tər) A place or object that protects an animal and keeps It safe. (p. A44)

silt (silt) Soil that is made of tiny rocks. *Silt* is carried by water and deposited as sediment. (p. C14)

simple machine (sim′pəl mə shēn′) A machine with few or no moving parts. (p. E44)

soil (soil) A mixture of tiny rock particles, minerals, and decayed plant and animal materials. (p. C14)

solar system (sō′lər sis′təm) The Sun and all the objects that orbit the Sun. (p. D54)

solid (sol′id) Matter that has a definite shape and volume. (p. F14)

solution (sə lü′shən) A kind of mixture in which one or more types of matter are mixed evenly in another kind of matter. (p. F19)

speed (spēd) How fast an object moves over a certain distance. (p. E9)

sphere (sfîr) A body that has the shape of a ball or globe. (p. D36)

spore (spôr) One of the tiny reproductive bodies of ferns and mosses, similar to the seeds of other plants. (p. A30)

star (stär) A huge, hot sphere of gases, like the Sun, that gives off its own light. (p. D55)

stem (stem) A plant part that supports the plant. (p. A17)

switch (swich) A lever that opens or closes an electric circuit. (p. F73)

system (sis'təm) A group of parts that work together. (p. A62)

texture (teks'chər) How the surface of an object feels to the touch. (p. F6)

thermometer (thər mom'ə tər) An instrument used to measure temperature. (pp. D8, D24)

tissue (tish'ü) A group of cells that are alike. (p. A62)

tornado (tôr nā'dō) A violent, whirling wind that moves across the ground in a narrow path. (p. C70)

tuber (tü'bər) The underground stem of a plant such as the potato. (p. A30)

tundra (tun'drə) A cold dry place. (p. B55)

 T

 U

telescope (tel'ə skōp') A tool that gathers light to make faraway objects appear closer. (p. D58)

temperature (tem'pər ə cher) How hot or cold something is. (pp. D8, F43)

use numbers (ūz num'bərz) To order, count, add, subtract, multiply, and divide to explain data. (p. S7)

use variables (ūz vâr'ē ə bəlz) To identify and separate things in an experiment that can be changed or controlled. (p. S7)

PRONUNCIATION KEY

a at; ā ape; ä far; âr care; ô law; e end; ē me; i it; ī ice; îr pierce; o hot; ō old; ôr fork; oi oil; ou out; u up; ū use; ü rule; ů pull; ûr turn; hw white; ng song; th thin; <u>th</u> this; zh measure; ə about, taken, pencil, lemon, circus

V

valley (val′ē) An area of low land lying between hills or mountains. (p. C55)

vibrate (vī′brāt) To move back and forth quickly. (p. F64)

volcano (vol kā′nō) An opening in the surface of Earth. (p. C73)

volume (vol′ūm) **1.** A measure of how much space matter takes up. (p. F7) **2.** How loud or soft a sound is. (p. F67)

W

water cycle (wô′tər sī′kəl) The movement of Earth's water over and over from a liquid to a gas and from a gas to a liquid. (pp. C31, D19)

water vapor (wô′tər vā′pər) Water in the form of a gas in Earth's atmosphere. (p. D17)

weather (weth′ər) The condition of the atmosphere at a given time and place. (p. D6)

weather vane (weth′ər vān) A device that indicates the direction of the wind. (p. D25)

weathering (weth′ər ing) The process that causes rocks to crumble, crack, and break. (p. C60)

wedge (wej) Two inclined planes placed back to back. (p. E55)

weight (wāt) The measure of the pull of gravity between an object and Earth. (p. E17)

wheel and axle (hwēl and ak′səl) A wheel that turns on a post. (p. E47)

wind (wind) Moving air. (p. D10)

windlass (wind′ləs) A wheel and axle machine that is turned by a hand crank to lift a bucket in a well. (p. E47)

work (wûrk) The force that changes the motion of an object. (p. E38)

Index

* Indicates an activity related to this topic.

* Indicates an activity related to this topic.

Explore activities – Inferring

F

G

H

I

* Indicates an activity related to this topic.

* Indicates an activity related to this topic.

Q

R

* Indicates an activity related to this topic.

* Indicates an activity related to this topic.

Credits

Page placement key: (t) top, (tr) top right, (tl) top left, (tm) top middle, (tml) top middle left, (tmr) top middle right, (m) middle, (l) left, (ml) middle left,(r) right, (mr) middle right,(b) bottom, (br) bottom right,(bl) bottom left, (bm) bottom middle, (bml) bottom middle left, (bmr) bottom middle right, (bg) background, (i) inset, (ti) top inset, (bi) bottom inset

Cover Design and Illustration: Robert Brook Allen

Cover Photos: Kim Taylor/Bruce Coleman/Natural Selection, (bg) Darrell Gulin/Stone, (l) © PhotoSpin 2000

Illustrations: Dolores Bego: p. E10; Frank Comito: p. R6; Barbara Cousins: pp. E21, R25, R27, (l) R28, R29; Daniel DelValle: p. B5; Jeff Fagen: pp. E27, E33; Function Through Form: p. F29; Peter Gunther: pp. C14,C26, C30, C31, C33, C61, C73, D7, D8, D10, D18, D31, D40, D42, E17, F8, F15, F42, F57, F63, F72; Colin Hayes: pp. A41, E44, E48, E48, E54, E55, E60, E61, R5, R7, R9, R16, R17, R18, (l) R19; John Karapelou: pp. R30, R32, (m) R33, (b) R33; Yuan Lee: B7, B8, B16, F68, F77; Tom Leonard: pp. R20,R21, R22, R23; Kevin O'Malley: pp. E25, F10, F11; Joe LeMonnier: pp. B64, C56, D11, D13, D26, D36, D37, D47, D61; Steve Oh: pp. A62, R26, R27, (r) R28, R29, R31, R34; Sharon O'Neil: p. C47; Precision Graphics: pp. A28, A29, A42, A71; Pat Rasch: pp. E56, E57, E58; Molly Scanlon: pp. F7, F64, F66, F74; Rob Schuster: p. F73; Neecy Twinem: pp. B10, B20; Olivia: pp. R2, R3, R9, R10, R11, R14, R15, (r) R19, Patricia Wynne: pp. S4, S5, R24, (t) R33; J/B Woolsey Associates: pp. A10, A11, C54, C76; Josie Yee: pp. D38, D54;

Photography Credits: All photographs are by the Macmillan/McGraw-Hill School Division (MMSD) and Michael Groen, Dan Howell, Ken Karp, Dave Mager, John Serafin for MMSD except as noted below.

Contents: iv: Photodisc. v: (l) Runk/Schoenberger/Grant Heilman Photography, Inc.; (r) Photodisc. vi: (l) Francois Gohier/Photo Researchers, Inc.; (r) American Museum of Natural History. vii: (l) NASA/Photo Researchers, Inc.; (r) John Sanford/Photo Researchers, Inc. viii: Peter Weimann/Animals Animals. ix: D. Boone/Corbis.

National Geographic Invitation to Science: S1: (bg) Greig Cranna/Stock • Boston; (i) Mark A. Madison. S2: Mark A. Madison. S3: (t) NASA/Peter Arnold Inc.; (b) Mark A. Madison. S7: Ken Karp. S8: (br) PhotoDisc.

National Geographic Unit Opener A: A0: Clive Druett/Papilio/Corbis. A1: Victoria McCormick/Animals Animals. **Unit A:** A2: Alan Oddie/PhotoEdit. A4: Douglas Peebles/Corbis. A5: Ken Karp. A6: (t) Terry Eggers/The Stock Market; (l) Tony Wharton/Corbis; (r) The Stock Market; (b) Terry Eggers/The Stock Market. A7: (t) Frank Siteman/Stock • Boston; (tr) Photodisc; (mr) Photodisc; (br) Photodisc. A8: (t) Gerard Fuehrer/DRK Photo; SuperStock. A9: (tl) Norbert Wu/Peter Arnold Inc.; (tr) Secret Sea Visions/Peter Arnold Inc.; (b) Joe McDonald/Visuals Unlimited. A10: (t) Kent Wood/Photo Researchers, Inc.; (b) Dwight R. Kuhn. A11: (t) Ken Karp; (b) Moredun Animal Health LTD/Science Photo Library/Photo Researchers, Inc. A12: Ken Karp. A13: Cart Roessler/Animals Animals. A14: (bg) PhotoDisc.; (tl) Doug Peebles/Panoramic Images; (tr) Allen Prier/Panoramic Images; (m) Mark Segal/Panoramic Images. A15: Ken Karp. A16: (bg) Runk/Schoenberger/Grant Heilman Photography; (i) E. Webber/Visuals Unlimited. A17: (l) Jim Zipp/Photo Researchers, Inc.; (r) Jenny Hager/The Image Works. A18: (l) Runk/Schoenberger/Grant Heilman Photography; (r) C.G. Van Dyke/Visuals Unlimited. A19: (t) Dave M. Phillips/Visuals Unlimited; (b) Ken Karp. A20: (t) Bill Beatty/Visuals Unlimited; (b) Pat O'Hara/DRK Photo. A22: (bg) Randy Green/FPG International; (l) Stan Osolinski/Dembinsky Photo Assoc.; (r) Larry West/FPG International. A23: (t) John M. Roberts/The Stock Market; (b) J. H. Robinson/Photo Researchers, Inc. A24: Neil Gilchrist/Panoramic Images. A25: Ken Karp. A26: (t) D. Gavagnaro/Visuals Unlimited; (tm) Kevin Collins/Visuals Unlimited; (bm) Tony Freeman/PhotoEdit; (bl) Inga Spence/Tom Stack & Associates; (br) Inga Spence/Visuals Unlimited. A27: D. Gavagnaro/Visuals Unlimited. A29: Gerald and Buff Corsi/Visuals Unlimited. A30: (t) David Young-Wolfe/PhotoEdit; (m) David Young-Wolfe/PhotoEdit; (bl) Ed Reschke/Peter Arnold Inc.; (br) Jeff J. Daly/Visuals Unlimited. A31: Inga Spence/Visuals Unlimited. A32: Ed Galindo. A33: (t) Ed Galindo; (b) C Squared Studios/PhotoDisc. A36: Stephen J. Krasemann/Photo Researchers, Inc. A38: Jade Albert/FPG International. A39: Ken Karp. A40: (t) Fritz Polikng/Bruce Coleman Inc.; (bl) Joe McDonald/DRK Photo; (br) Dale E. Boyer/Photo Researchers, Inc. A41: Kevin Schafer/Peter Arnold Inc. A42: (i) W. Gregory Brown/Animals Animals; (v) Michael S. Nolan/Tom Stack & Associates. A43: Ken Karp. A44: (t) Eric & David Hosking/Corbis; (m) John Cancalosi/DRK Photo; (b) Ted Levine/Animals Animals. A45: (t) Zoran Milich/Allsport USA; (b) Mark Newman/Bruce

Coleman Inc. A46: (t) David Madison/Bruce Coleman Inc.; (m) Runk/Schoenberger/Grant Heilman Photography; (b) John Cancalosi/DRK Photo. A48: (bg) Ken Lucas/Visuals Unlimited; (t) Skip Moody/Dembinsky Photo Assoc.; (b) Skip Moody/Dembinsky Photo Assoc. A49: (tl) Skip Moody/Dembinsky Photo Assoc.; (tr) Skip Moody/Dembinsky Photo Assoc.; (b) Jon Dicus; (b) Skip Moody/Dembinsky Photo Assoc. A50: Tim Davis/Photo Researchers, Inc. A51: Ken Karp. A52: (t) Dwight R. Kuhn; (b) Arthur Morris/Visuals Unlimited. A53: (tl) Gelnn M. Oliver/Visuals Unlimited; (tr) Robert P. Carr/Bruce Coleman Inc.; (tm) Pat Lynch/Zipp/Photo Researchers, Inc.; (ml) Nuridsany et Perennou/Zipp/Photo Researchers, Inc.; (mr) Robert L. Dunne/Bruce Coleman Inc.; (bl) Sharon Cummings/Dembinsky Photo Assoc.; (br) John Mielcarek/Dembinsky Photo Assoc. A54: (t) SuperStock; (mr) Lynn Rogers/Peter Arnold Inc.; (bl) Erwin and Peggy Bauer/Bruce Coleman Inc.; (br) Pat and Tom Leeson/Photo Researchers, Inc. A55: (t) Cabisco/Visuals Unlimited; (ml) E.A. Janes/Bruce Coleman Inc; (mr) Lindholm/Visuals Unlimited; (bm) Fred Breummer/DRK Photo; (bl) M H Sharp/Photo Researchers, Inc; (br) Dave B. Fleetham/Visuals Unlimited. A56: (t) Ken Karp; (bl) George Shelley/The Stock Market; (br) Richard Hutchings/PhotoEdit. A58: (bg) J.C. Carton/Bruce Coleman Inc.; (i) Bill Banaszewski/Visuals Unlimited. A60: Robert Maier/Animals Animals. A61: Ken Karp. A62: (t) Ken Karp; (b) M.I. Walker/Science Source/Photo Researchers, Inc. A63: (t) R. Dowling/Animals Animals; (b) Joe McDonald/Animals Animals. A64: (t) Robert Winslow; (b) Tom Brakefield/Corbis. A65: (t) James Watt/Animals Animals; (b) Jeff Rotman/Jeff Rotman Photography. A66: Photodisc. A68: VCG/FPG International. A69: (t) Stephen Dalton/Animals Animals; (tm) Tony Wharton/Corbis; (mm) G.W.Willis/Animals Animals; (ml) Eye Wire; (mr) Brian Parker/Tom Stack & Associates; (bl) Kichen and Hurst/Tom Stack & Associates; (br) Lisa and Mike Husar/DRK Photo. A70: (l) Darryl Torckler/Tony Stone Images; (r) Rob Simpson/Visuals Unlimited. A71: (i) George Bernard/Animals Animals; (r) Breck P. Kent/Animals Animals. A72: (t) Jane Borton/Bruce Coleman Inc.; (b) E.R. Degginger/Animals Animals. A73: (l) S. Nielson/DRK Photo; (r) Robert Winslow. A74: (t) Jeff Rotman/Jeff Rotman Photography; (b) Dave Watts/Tom Stack & Associates. A75: (t) Erwin & Peggy Bauer/Bruce Coleman Inc.; (b) Lynn M. Stone/Bruce Coleman Inc. A77: (l) SuperStock; (r) SuperStock. A78: (bg) Michael Fogden/DRK Photo; (i) Dr. Fransisco Gomez-Dallmeier. A80: (tl) David Young-Wolfe/PhotoEdit; (tr) Jeff J. Daly/Visuals Unlimited.

National Geographic Unit Opener B: B00: Tim Flach/Tony Stone. B0 Christer Fredriksson/Natural Selection Stock Photography. B1 Tim Davis/Tony Stone. **Unit B:** B2: (bg) Corbis; (l) John Gerlach/Visuals Unlimited; (m) David M. Schleser/Photo Researchers, Inc.; (r) Tony Stone Images. B4: Johnny Johnson/Animals Animals. B6: Photodisc. B6: (t) Nicholas DeVore/Tony Stone Images; (b) Joseph Van Os/Image Bank. B12: (i) Lance Nelson/The Stock Market; (m) Jeff Greenberg/Visuals Unlimited; (b) Jeff Greenberg/PhotoEdit. B13: (i) PhotoDisc; (t) Gerard Lacz/Peter Arnold Inc.; (b) PhotoDisc. B14: (bg) L. Lenz/Natural Selection. B16: Kim Taylor/Dorling Kindersley Ltd. B18: (i) Runk/Schoenberger /Grant Heilman Photography; (t) SuperStock; (bl) Tom Bean/DRK Photo; (br) Kim Taylor/Dorling Kindersley Ltd. B19: (l) Michael P. Gadomski/Photo Researchers, Inc. B22: (t) John Warden/Tony Stone Images; (tm) Tom J. Ulrich/Visuals Unlimited; (bm) John Shaw/Bruce Coleman Inc; (b) Runk/Schoenberger/Grant Heilman Photography, Inc. B23: Jim Steinberg/Photo Researchers, Inc. B24: (bg) Michael Simpson/FPG International. B26: (bg) Kent Foster/Photo Researchers, Inc; (i) William H. Mullins/Photo Researchers, Inc. B28: (ti) John Shaw/Bruce Coleman Inc.; (t) Kim Taylor/Dorling Kindersley Ltd.; (tm) Kim Taylor/Dorling Kindersley Ltd.; (ml) Arthur Morris/The Stock Market.; (mr) M. C. Chamberlain/DRK Photo; (b) Kim Taylor/Dorling Kindersley Ltd. B29: (t) Jeremy Woodhouse/PhotoDisc; (b) Jerry Young/Dorling Kindersley Ltd. B30: (tl) Nawrocki Stock Photo; (b) Carl Roessler/Bruce Coleman Inc. B31: (tr) S. Dimmitt/Photo Researchers, Inc; (m) James H. Robinson/Photo Researchers, Inc; (bl) Tony Stone Images; (br) Runk/Schoenberger/Grant Heilman Photography, Inc. B32: (r) Kim Taylor/Dorling Kindersley Ltd. B34: (bg) John Elk III; (ti) Trevor Barrett/Earth Scenes; (bi) George D. Lepp/Photo Researchers, Inc. B35: Kjell B. Sandved/Visuals Unlimited. B37: (l) Runk/Schoenberger/Grant Heilman Photography, Inc.; (m) Runk/Schoenberger/Grant Heilman Photography, Inc; (r) Arthur Morris/Visuals Unlimited. B38: Robert Winslow. B40: (bg) The Stock Market. B42: (t) Stephen Dalton/Animals Animals; (b) Richard Day/Panoramic Images. B43: (tl) Steve Maslowski/Visuals Unlimited; (tr) James P. Rowan/DRK Photo; (tr) George D. Dodge/Bruce Coleman Inc.; (mr) Michael Dwyer/Stock • Boston. B44: (t) Gail Shumway/FPG International; (b) Ken Karp. B45: (l) Ken Lax/Photo Researchers, Inc. B46: (t) M.L. Sinibaldi/The Stock Market; (b) H.P. Merten/The Stock Market. B47: Larry Ulrich/DRK Photo. B48: (bg) Johnny Johnson/DRK Photo; (t) Tom and Pat Leeson/DRK Photo; (b) Richard &Susan Day/Animals Animals. B50: (t) Gail Shumway/FPG International; (m) Jack Jeffrey/Photo Resource Hawaii.; (b) John Cancalosi/DRK Photo. B51: (tl) Francis/Donna

Caldwell/Visuals Unlimited; (tr) Jack Hollingsworth/Photodisc; (b) Kim Taylor/Bruce Coleman Inc. B52: (t) Gregory Ochoki/Photo Researchers, Inc.; (b) Breck P. Kent/Animals Animals. B53: (t) Stephen J. Krasemann/DRK Photo; (m) A. Cosmos Blank/Photo Researchers, Inc.; (b) John Eastcott/Yva Momatiuk/DRK Photo. B54: (t) Zig Leszcynski/Animals Animals; (m) MIchael Fogden/DRK Photo; (b) MIchael Fogden/DRK Photo. B55: (tl) Pat O'Hara/DRK Photo; (tr) Richard Kolar/Animals Animals; (tm) Don Enger/Animals Animals; (bl) Jim Steinberg/Photo Researchers, Inc.; (br) Stephen J. Krasemann/Photo Researchers, Inc. B56: Ken Karp. B57: Chris Johns/National Geographic. B58: (bg) Gary Braasch/Corbis. B59: Ken Karp. B60: (t) Charles Palek/Earth Scenesphic; (b) Pat and Tom Lesson/Photo Researchers, Inc. B61: (l) Robert Madden/National Geographicphic; (r) James Hughes/Visuals Unlimited. B62: (t) Diana L. Stratton/Tom Stack & Associates; (tm) Doug Sokell/Visuals Unlimited; (l) Kent and Donna Dannen/Photo Researchers, Inc.; (bm) Sharon Gerig/Tom Stack & Associates; (b) Pat and Tom Lesson/DRK Photo. B63: (t) Joe & Carol McDonald/Visuals Unlimited; (b) Stephen J. Krasemann/DRK Photo. B64: (t) M.C. Chamberlain/DRK Photo; (bl) Erwin and Peggy Bauer/Bruce Coleman Inc.; (br) G. Prance/Visuals Unlimited. B65: (b) M.C. Chamberlain/DRK Photo. B66: (t) Stephen J. Krasemann/DRK Photo; (b) Science VU/Visuals Unlimited. B67: (t) Barbara Gerlach/Visuals Unlimited. B69: (l) Pat and Tom Lesson/Photo Researchers, Inc.; (r) Robert Madden/National Geographic. B70: (t) Christina Allen. B71: Myleen Ferguson/PhotoEdit.

National Geographic Unit Opener C: C0: Donovan Reese/Tony Stone. C1: David Muench/Tony Stone. **Unit C:** C2: David Muench/Corbis. C4: (bg) Chip Porter/Tony Stone Images. C5: Ken Karp. C6: (t) Joyce Photographics/Photo Researchers, Inc.; (m) Runk/Schoenberger/Grant Heilman Photography; (b) Bill Bachmann/Index Stock Imagery. C7: (t) Tom Pantages; (m) Tom Pantages; (b) Ken Karp. C8: Adam G. Sylvester/Photo Researchers, Inc. C9: (tl) Ken Karp; (tr) S. Callahan/Visuals Unlimited; (tml) Joyce Photographics/Photo Researchers, Inc.; (tmr) Runk/Schoenberger/Grant Heilman Photography; (bl) Charles R. Belinky/Photo Researchers, Inc.; (br) Ken Karp. C10: (t) Frederik D. Bodin/Stock • Boston; (m) Erich Lessing/Art Resource; (b) Boleslaw Edelhajt/Gamma-Liaison. C12: (bg) Bo Brannhage/Panoramic Images. C13: Ken Karp. C14: Larry Lefever/Grant Heilman Photography. C15: (l) Stephen Ogilvy; (m) Ken Karpgilvy; (r) Ken Karp. C16: Ken Karp. C17: (l) George Lepp/Corbis; (r) Runk/Schoenberger/Grant Heilman Photography. C18: (tl) Roy Morsch/The Stock Market; (tr) Roy Morsch/The Stock Market; (m) The National Archives/Corbis; (bm) Roy Morsch/The Stock Market; (b) G. Buttner/Okapia/Photo Researchers, Inc. C19: Arthur C. Smith/Grant Heilman Photography. C20: (b) Jeff J. Daly/Visuals Unlimited. C21: Ken Karp. C22: Tom Bean/DRK Photo. C23: (t) Runk/Schoenberger/Grant Heilman Photography; (b) Ken Karp. C24: (i) Mehau Kulyk/Photo Researchers, Inc.; (t) Louis Psihoyos/Matrix; (b) Fracois Gohier/Photo Researchers, Inc. C25: (l) Stephen J. Krasemann/DRK Photo; (m) Biophoto Associates/Photo Researchers, Inc.; (r) Stephen J. Krasemann/DRK Photo. C26: Ray Ellis/Photo Researchers, Inc. C28: (bg) F. Stuart Westmorland/Photo Researchers, Inc. C29: Ken Karp. C30: Tom Van Sant/Photo Researchers, Inc. C32: (t) Davis Barber/PhotoEdit; (b) C. C. Lockwood/DRK Photo. C35: John Serafin. C36: (bg) Grant Heilman/Grant Heilman Photography. C37: Ken Karp. C38: (bl) Charles Mauzy/Natural Selection; (br) Emma Lee/Life File/Photodisc. C39: (t) David R. Frazier/Photo Researchers, Inc.; (b) John Elk III. C40: (t) Don and Pat Valenti/DRK Photo; (b) Gary Gray/DRK Photo. C41: (i) Will and Deni McIntyre/Photo Researchers, Inc.; (t) American Museum of Natural History; (b) George Gerster/Photo Researchers, Inc. C42: (t) Ruth Dixon/Stock • Boston; (b) David Ulmer/Stock • Boston. C43: (l) Simon Fraser/Science Photo Library/Photo Researchers, Inc.; (r) Ken Karp. C44: (tl) Larry Lefever/Grant Heilman Photography; (tml) Eye Wire; (bml) R.J. Erwin/DRK Photo; (bl) Tony Freeman/PhotoEdit; (br) Hutchings Photography. C45: (l) Michael P. Gadomski/Photo Researchers, Inc. C46: (t) David Young-Wolfe/PhotoEdit; (b) Chromosohm/Sohm/Stock • Boston. C47: (t) Bonnie Kaman/PhotoEdit; (t) Spencer Grant/PhotoEdit. C50: Addison Geary/Stock • Boston. C52: (bg) Allen Prier/Panoramic Images. C53: (t) Peter Miller/Panoramic Images; (tm) Richard Sisk/Panoramic Images; (m) Mark Heifner/Panoramic Images; (bm) Kim Heacox/Tony Stone Images; (bl) Jack Krawczyk/Panoramic Images; (br) Don Pitcher/Stock • Boston. C56: (tl) Jim Wiebe/Panoramic Images; (tr) Peter Pearson/Tony Stone Images; (bm) Mark Heifner/Panoramic Images; (bl) Richard Sisk/Panoramic Images; (br) Tom Bean/Tony Stone Images. C57: Jack Krawczyk/Panoramic Images. C58: (bg) David L. Brown/Panoramic Images. C59: Ken Karp. C60: (t) Michael P. Gadomski/Photo Researchers, Inc.; (b) John Anderson/Earth Scenes. C61: Ken Karp. C62: (i) Photodisc; (t) Thomas Fletcher/Stock • Boston; (b) Jeff Greenberg/PhotoEdit. C63: (t) Kathy Ferguson/PhotoEdit; (b) Runk/Schoenberger/Grant Heilman Photography. C64: Ken Karp. C65: PhotoEdit. C66: (bg) The National Archives/Corbis; (i) Adam

Jones/Photo Researchers, Inc.; (t) W. E. Ruth/Bruce Coleman Inc. C67: (i) Pat Armstrong/Visuals Unlimited; (m) Sylvan H. Wittaver/Visuals Unlimited; (b) John Sohlden/Visuals Unlimited. C68: (bg) David Young-Wolfe/PhotoEdit. C69: Ken Karp. C70: (t) Ana Laura Gonzalez/Earth Scenes; (b) Art Montes De Oca/FPG International. C72: (t) David Bartruff/FPG International; (b) Will & Deni McIntyre/Photo Researchers, Inc. C73: G. Brad Lewis/Tony Stone Images. C74: (t) David Weintraub/Stock • Boston; (b) Archive photos/Library of Congress. C78: (bg) Fred Bavendam/Peter Arnold Inc.; (t) Dawn Wright/Dawn Wright; (b) Peter Ryan/Scripps Science Photo Library/Photo Researchers, Inc. C79: Mark M. Lawrence/The Stock Market.

National Geographic Unit Opener D: D00: Earth Satellite Corporation/Science Photo Library/Photo Researchers, Inc. D0 John Sanford/Science Photo Library/Photo Researchers, Inc D1: Science Photo Library/Photo Researchers, Inc; Photo Library Int'l/Photo Researchers, Inc. **Unit D:** D2: Jack Krawczyk/Panoramic Images. D4: (bg) Ariel Skelley/The Stock Market. D5: Ken Karp. D6: Ken Karp. D9: (l) Didier Givois/Photo Researchers, Inc.; (r) Ken Karp. D10: David Young-Wolfe/Photo Researchers, Inc. D11: Barbara Stotzen/PhotoEdit. D12: Paul & LindaMarie Ambrose/FPG International. D13: Howard Bluestein/Photo Researchers, Inc. D14: (bg) Clifford Paine/Corbis. D15: Ken Karp. D16: (t) Myrleen Ferguson/PhotoEdit; (m) Paul Silverman/Paul Silverman; (b) Michael Newman/PhotoEdit. D17: (t) Diane Hirsch/Fundamental Photographs; (b) Jeff Greenberg/Peter Arnold Inc. D20: Ken Karp. D21: P. Quittemelle/Stock • Boston. D22: (bg) Bob Krist/Corbis. D23: Dave Mager. D24: (tr) Tom Pantages; (l) Tom Pantages; (br) Jeff J. Daly/Stock • Boston. D25: (t) Charles D. Winters/Photo Researchers, Inc.; (br) Ken Karp; (bl) Tony Freeman/PhotoEdit. D27: (b) NOAA/Science photo Library/Photo Researchers, Inc. D28: (t) Michael P. Gadomski/Photo Researchers, Inc.; (b) Michael P. Gadomski/Photo Researchers, Inc. D29: F. Stuart Westmorland/Photo Researchers, Inc. D32: Michael Hovell/Index Stock Imagery. D34: (bg) Robert Mathena/Fundamental Photographs. D35: Ken Karp. D37: (t) Ken Lucas/Visuals Unlimited; (b) Thomas Barbudo/Panoramic Images. D40: Ken Karp. D41: Bob Daemmrich/Stock • Boston. D42: Jim Ballard/All Stock/PNI; David Nunuk/Science Photo Library/Photo Researchers, Inc. D44: (bg) Peter Menzel/Stock • Boston. D45: Ken Karp. D46: John R. Foster/Photo Researchers, Inc. D47: John Sanford/Photo Researchers, Inc. D48: NASA/Science Source/Photo Researchers, Inc. D49: (l) Mark E. Gibson/Visuals Unlimited; (r) NASA/Science Photo Library/Photo Researchers, Inc. D52: (bg) Frank Zullo/Photo Researchers, Inc. D53: Ken Karp. D56: (t) U.S .Geological Survey/Photo Researchers, Inc; (m) NASA/Mark Marten/Photo Researchers, Inc.; (bl) Stock • Boston; (br) NASA/Tom Pantages. D57: (tl) Ross Ressmeyer/NASA/Corbis; (tr) NASA/Photo Researchers, Inc.; (ml) Space Telescope Space Institute/Photo Researchers, Inc.; (mr) NASA/Tom Pantages. D57: (b) Space Telescope Space Institute/Photo Researchers, Inc. D58: (t) Tony Freeman/PhotoEdit; (b) Ken Karp. D62: (bg) Pekka Parvaiainen/Science Photo Library/Photo Researchers, Inc.; (i) Seth Shostak/Seth Shostak. D63: Seth Shostak/Seth Shostak. D64: Ken Karp.

National Geographic Unit Opener E: E0: James Marshall/The Stock Market. E1: Ron Stroud/Masterfile. **Unit E:** E2: Bernard Asset/Photo Researchers, Inc. E4: (bg) S. Dalton/Photo Researchers, Inc. E5: (t) Will Hart/PhotoEdit; (b) Ken Karp. E6: (t) Gregory K. Scott/Photo Researchers, Inc.; (tr) Foodpix; (ml) Gregory K. Scott/Photo Researchers, Inc.; (mr) Foodpix; (bl) Zoran Milich/Allsport USA; (br) Zoran Milich/Allsport USA. E7: (t) Ken Karp; (b) Ken Karp. E8: (bg) The Stock Market; (t) Robert Winslow; (b) Fritz Polking/Peter Arnold Inc. E9: (t) Joseph Van Os/Image Bank; (b) Peter Weimann/Animals Animals. E12: (bg) Craig J. Brown/Flashfocus. E16: (l) NASA; (r) Hutchings Photography. E17: NASA/Earth Scenes. E18: Photodisc. E19: (t) Art Resource. E20: Ken Karp. E23: (i) Ken Karp. E26: (i) Tony Freeman/PhotoEdit; (b) John Coletti/Stock • Boston. E27: Bob Daemmrich/Stock • Boston. E28: (r) Ken Karp. E30: (bg) Hulton Getty; (l) Michael Conroy/AP World Wide Photos. E31: (t) UPI/Corbis/Bettman; (b) Courtesy of Speedo. E34: Addison Geary/Stock • Boston. E38: (tl) David Young-Wolfe/PhotoEdit; (tr) Hutchings Photography; (bl) Hutchings Photography; (br) John Eastcott/YvaMomatiuk/DRK Photo. E39: (r) Ken Karp; David Matherly/Visuals Unlimited. E42: (bg) Bob Daennrich/Stock • Boston. E43: Ken Karp. E45: Ken Karp. E46: (tm) Michael Newman/PhotoEdit; (m) Tony Freeman/PhotoEdit; (b) Siede Preis/Photodisc. E47: (t) Roger Wilmshurst; Frank Lane Picture Agency/Corbis; (m) Corbis; (b) Eric Roth/Flashfocus. E48: Ken Karp. E49: (t) Domenicho Fetti/The Granger Collection. E50: (l) Joan Iaconetti/Bruce Coleman Inc.; (r) David Mager. E51: David Mager. E52: (bg) McCutchean/Visuals Unlimited. E54: Richard Hutchings/Photo Researchers, Inc. E55: Donald Specker/Earth Scenes. E56: Mark Burnett/Stock • Boston. E57: (t) Photodisc; (b) David Young-Wolfe/PhotoEdit. E59: Jodi Jacobson. E62: (bg) NASA/The Image Works; (i) Joe Skipper/Archive Photos/Reuters. E63: NASA. E64: (t) Ken Karp; (b) John Neubauer/PhotoEdit.

National Geographic Unit Opener F: F0: SuperStock. F1 Kunio Owaki/The Stock Market. **Unit F:** F2: Myrleen Ferguson/PhotoEdit; (i) Ken Karp; (r) Ken Karp. F6: (t) Hutchings Photography; (m) Photodisc; (ml) RDF/Visuals Unlimited; (mr) RDF/Visuals Unlimited. F7: (l) Spencer Grant/PhotoEdit; (m) Photodisc; (r) Diane Padys/FPG International; (b) Index Stock. F8: (l) Spencer Grant/PhotoEdit; (r) Diane Padys/FPG International. F10: (l) VCG/FPG International; (r) Stock • Boston. F12: (bg) Alan Kearney/FPG International. F13: Ken Karp. F14: (t) PhotoDisc; (bl) PhotoDisc; (br) Hutchings Photography. F15: (l) Hutchings Photography; (m) PhotoDisc; (r) PhotoDisc. F16: (i) Lawrence Migdale; (r) Lawrence Migdale; (b) David Young-Wolfe/PhotoEdit. F17: (tl) SuperStock; (tr) Hutchings Photography; (bl) Amanda Merullo/Stock • Boston; (br) SuperStock. F18: (t) PhotoDisc. F20: Peter Scoones/TCL/Masterfile. F21: (l) Tony Freeman/PhotoEdit. F22: (tl) Ken Karp; (tr) Norman Owen Tomalin/Bruce Coleman Inc.; (tml) Norman Owen Tomalin/Bruce Coleman Inc.; (tmr) Norman Owen Tomalin/Bruce Coleman Inc.; (m) Steve Kline/Bruce Coleman Inc.; (m) Ken Karp; (b) Ken Karp. F23: (t) Norman Owen Tomalin/Bruce Coleman Inc.; (b) Bruce Byers/FPG International. F24: (bg) Spencer Grant/PhotoEdit. F25: Ken Karp. F27: (t) Bo Brannhagen/Panoramic Images; (tm) Burke/Triolo Productions/Foodpix; (m) PhotoDisc; (b) Photodisc. F28: (t) D. Boone/Corbis; (b) Ken Karp. F29: The Stock Market. F30: (l) Photodisc; (m) Eye Wire; (r) PhotoDisc. F31: (bl) PhotoDisc. F32: (t) Ernie Friedlander/Flashfocus; (m) Fred J. Maroon/Photo Researchers, Inc.; (ml) Gabriel Covian/Image Bank; (mr) David Sieren/Visuals Unlimited; (bl) Barbara Stitzer/PhotoEdit. F34: (l) Joel Sartore/Grant Heilman Photography; (r) Leonard Lessin/Peter Arnold Inc.; (b) James L. Amos/Peter Arnold Inc. F35: Gabe Palmer/The Stock Market. F37: Tom Pantages; Richard Megna/Fundamental Photographs; Jerry Driendl/FPG International. F38: Glenn Vanstrum/Earth Scenes. F40: (bg) Tom Bean/DRK Photo; (i) Kim Fennema/Visuals Unlimited. F42: Hutchings Photography. F43: (ti) Hutchings Photography; (bi) Hutchings Photography; (r) Hutchings Photography; (b) Bill Bachmann/PhotoEdit. F44: (l) Hutchings Photography; (b) PhotoDisc. F45: Ken Karp. F46: (t) Jerry Driendl/FPG International; (l) SuperStock; (b) Image Bank. F47: (t) Renee Lynn/Photo Researchers, Inc.; (bl) Nakita Ovsyanikov/Masterfile; (br) SuperStock. F48: (t) Farrel Grehan/Photo Researchers, Inc.; (m) Hutchings Photography; (b) Ken Karp. F49: Nancy P. Alexander/Visuals Unlimited. F50: (bg) Travel Pix/FPG International; (t) Jerome Wexler/Photo Researchers, Inc.; (b) Adam Hart-Davis/Photo Researchers, Inc. F51: (t) Bob Daemmrich/Stock • Boston; (b) FPG International. F52: (bg) Kirchoff/Wohlberg. F53: Ken Karp. F54: (bg) Black Sheep. F55: (b) Gupton/Pictor/Entertainment. F56: (t) Charles D. Winters/Photo Researchers, Inc.; (bl) Hutchings Photography; (br) Photodisc. F57: (i) David Parker/Photo Researchers, Inc.; (b) SuperStock. F58: Ken Karp. F59: (l) Deborah Davis/PhotoEdit; (r) Peter Harholdt/SuperStock. F60: (t) Ken Karp; (t) Jim Cummins/FPG International; (b) Gerald French/FPG International. F61: Frank Krahmer/Bruce Coleman Inc. F62: (bg) Phyllis Picardi/International Stock. F63: Ken Karp. F64: (t) Ken Karp; (b) Spencer Grant/Stock • Boston. F65: (b) Telegraph Colour Library/FPG International. F66: (t) Bill Gallery/Stock • Boston; (b) Corbis. F67: (l) G K & Vikki Hart/Image Bank; (r) David Ducros/Science Photo Library. F68: (l) Chuck Carlton/Flashfocus; (r) Ken Cavanagh/Photo Researchers, Inc. F70: (bg) Chris Minerva/Index Stock Imagery. F71: Ken Karp. F72: Hutchings Photography. F74: (tl) Photodisc; (tr) Hutchings Photography; (ml) Will Crocker/Image Bank; (mr) Will Crocker/Image Bank; (bl) Stephen Marks/Image Bank; (br) Daniel Valdez. F78: (bg) Planet Earth Pictures/FPG International; (i) NASA. F79: Bill Horseman/Stock • Boston.

Science and Health Handbook: R4-R12: Stephen Ogilvy. R13: PhotoDisc. R28-R34: Hutchings Photography.